FAMILY SECRET

by Warren Robert Hull
with Michael B. Druxman

FAMILY SECRET
by Warren Robert Hull with Michael B. Druxman

Hughes Photo Credit — Herald Examiner Collection/Los Angeles Public Library.

Published in the USA by:
BearManor Media
4700 Millenia Blvd.
Suite 175 PMB 90497
Orlando, FL 32839
www.bearmanormedia.com

Paperback ISBN: 978-1-62933-552-0
Case ISBN: 978-1-62933-553-7
BearManor Media, Orlando, Florida
Printed in the United States of America
Book design by Robbie Adkins, www.adkinsconsult.com

Table of Contents

Acknowledgements

When I was first challenged to investigate the amazing details behind our *Family Secret*, I was a bit overwhelmed; the story specifics were so remarkable and so complex. I knew the task of writing this story was going to be gigantic. Had it not been for the support and inspiration of so many people, this story probably would have forever remained merely a family secret.

* * * * *

To Michael Druxman,

This was a story that needed to be told. Without your guidance, it may not have come to be. Thank you for your efforts.

To my father, Robert,

The last seven years have changed my life in ways I only came to understand after I had completed the journey you sent me on. I have grown in ways I never thought possible. Researching and then writing this story created a happening in my life much like the one Kevin Costner's character experienced in *Field of Dreams*. I knew that I had to build the ball field. I just wasn't sure why until the end of the tale. What I discovered in my cornfield wasn't what I'd anticipated. It was something much better.

To my mother, Marion,

Thank you for making the fuzzy things clear—not just with this story, but through my entire life. Your guidance and your willingness to explore and reveal long-hidden emotions allowed both of us to grow.

To my wife, Annette,

Thank you for being so many things. Thank you for your love, your patience, your understanding, and for taking this amazing journey of discovery with me. I could not have completed this pilgrimage without you.

To the MacDonald children,

The tragedy of losing your parents no doubt created a pain that very few can understand. My hope is you led happy, healthy and wonderful lives.

To Betty Ann Rockwell MacDonald,

I wish I would have had the opportunity to know you, but in many ways, after writing this book, I feel I have had that pleasure. I am saddened that you were taken from this world so soon. I have every confidence that, had you lived, you would have made a difference in many people's lives. As I learned about the elements of your life, my true spirit was awakened. As ironic as it sounds, your life has touched my soul in ways I am only just now beginning to comprehend. I can only hope that, by telling this tale, your spirit will be allowed to finally rest in peace.

Introduction

On the night that Benjamin "Bugsy" Siegel met his end, I was six years old, living in Seattle, Washington, fast asleep in my bed. In fact, I was a teenager before I'd even heard of Bugsy Siegel.

Like my father, I loved gangster movies. Bogart, Cagney, Eddie Robinson, Broderick Crawford, and George Raft were my idols. I saw all their movies and devoured stories about them in the fan magazines.

Raft, during the 1950s, published an autobiography in the *Saturday Evening Post*, and it was in that multi-part piece that I first saw Siegel's name and learned about his killing. Raft and Siegel had been friends from childhood, and as I recall, according to the article, the actor had been with him either the day of or the day before his demise. After I came to Hollywood, I got to know Raft; lunched with him once or twice...but we never spoke of Siegel.

In 1974, I lived in the Oak Park neighborhood of Agoura Hills, California. One of my neighbors was a man named Eddie Cannizzaro. He lived with his mother and was known in the neighborhood as the "cat man," because every evening at six, he would go to a particular corner and feed all the felines in the area. He was also known to have once been connected to the Mob, but he claimed that he was a mere bookkeeper.

My first book had just been published, which made me something of a neighborhood celebrity. One day, Eddie stopped by my house and asked if I would like to write a book with him about his experiences in the Mob. Initially, I wasn't very interested because, after the success of *The Godfather* two years earlier, there had been dozens of books and movies about the Mafia, and I felt that the subject had, for the time being, been pretty well played out.

"What if the book contained some sensational revelations?" Eddie asked.

"Like what?"

"That I'm the guy who pulled the trigger on Bugsy Siegel."

After I'd recovered from my surprise, Eddie proceeded to sketch out the details of the assassination.

"Do you really want to do this?" I asked him.

"Why not?"

"Because there's no statute of limitations on murder."

Long pause.

"Maybe I'd better think that over," he said, heading for the door. Then, he turned back to me and said, "You're not going to say anything about this, are you?"

I assured him that my lips were sealed, and he left. We never spoke of the subject again, though over the years, I occasionally related the story at dinner parties or in private. Eddie died in 1987, and it's my understanding that he made a deathbed confession to a newspaper reporter.

Ten years later, on the fiftieth anniversary of Siegel's murder, the *Los Angeles Times* ran a long article on the case, in which the Cannizzaro confession was mentioned. In response, I wrote a letter to the paper in which I related my Cannizzaro story. The *Times* ran the piece, and that's when it all began.

Suddenly, I was deluged with phone calls. CNN and E! both came out to my home in Calabasas, where I was then living, and did interviews with me. I even got a call from a detective with the Beverly Hills Police Department, who wanted me to go over my Cannizzaro story with him, piece by piece. For the BHPD, the Bugsy Siegel murder is still an open case.

I asked the homicide detective, Les Zoeller, what he thought of Cannizzaro's story. His response was: "If he didn't do it, then he was either there or knows somebody who was, because he knew some things that only the killer could have known."

Whether I'm writing a novel or a non-fiction book, writing and/or directing a stage play or film, I'm a storyteller. That's my profession, and I suddenly realized that there were one or more great stories to be gleaned from my experience with Eddie Cannizzaro.

I did two things. First, I wrote a screenplay, *Bugsy's Boys*, a partly-fact/mostly-fiction action-comedy, based on my encounter with Cannizzaro. At this writing, the script has not yet been produced, though a couple of well-known names, including an Oscar-winner, have indicated that they would like to play the Cannizzaro role. Second, I published my letter to the *Times* on the Internet, stating that I wanted to write a non-fiction account about the Siegel murder, and if there was anybody out there who knew what *really* happened that fatal night in Beverly Hills, to please e-mail me.

A month or two later, I received an e-mail from Warren Hull, an assistant athletic director and football coach from the University of Wisconsin. He claimed to know who killed Siegel and how it came about.

At first, I was quite dubious about Hull's story, because it appeared to contradict what Eddie Cannizzaro had told me. However, as I pondered his version, I recalled what Detective Zoeller had said about Cannizzaro's confession: "If he didn't do it, then *he was either there or knows somebody who was*, because he knew some things that only the killer could have known."

Certainly, Hull's story fit within these parameters, so I put him in touch with Detective Zoeller, who agreed with me that it was a very credible version of what might have happened to Siegel…but there was one problem. Convincing as it might be, all of Hull's evidence was circumstantial. There was no tangible proof to support his story, no "smoking gun."

I had a decision to make. Warren Hull wanted me to help him write his story, both as a book and a screenplay. Did I believe what he'd told me?

Ultimately, I decided that he believed it. He'd heard the story from his late father, shortly before his death, who claimed that he'd unknowingly supplied the murder weapon to the killer. Hull's mother had confirmed this and many of the other facts to him. Based on my belief that Warren Hull is an honorable man, I decided to proceed with the project.

Besides, true or false, it was a great story, and as I told you before, storytelling is my profession.

—Michael B. Druxman

Chapter One
A Skeleton Goes Into the Closet

September 13, 1947

On the last day of her life, Betty Ann Rockwell MacDonald arose early. She enjoyed the solitude daybreak brought, the crispness of the morning air, and the birds' sunrise serenades.

Upon going downstairs, she immediately noticed that the aroma of freshly brewed coffee filled the air. Constance Baker, the family housekeeper, had already started her day.

Betty Ann poured herself a large cup, then exited the house and headed for the backyard pool. She sat there for a half-hour, watching the start of the new day. She had come to enjoy these times, as every sunrise confirmed to her the joy that came from new beginnings. This morning was particularly exciting, for today was going to be a turning point in her life.

Betty Ann finished her coffee and began tending to her flower garden. The garden had become a place for her to find some much-needed solitude, no matter what nightmares the previous evening had brought.

Looking about at all the blossoms in her sanctuary, she quickly found the perfect type of flower for this day's centerpiece—roses, white and red roses. The rose had become Betty Ann's favorite flower, and long ago, she had come to appreciate the simple beauty and elegance that the rose possessed. Ironically, the qualities Betty Ann seemed to admire most in the flower were also a reflection of who, and what, Betty Ann had become—a woman of simple beauty and elegance.

Back in the house, Betty Ann refashioned and placed her centerpiece on the kitchen table. She stood back and peacefully admired her effort.

Mrs. Baker returned from the market, carrying a bag of groceries. As she came into the kitchen, she looked at Betty Ann's creation. Without taking her eyes off the flowers, she set the bags down on the counter and commented, "What a pleasurable start to the day."

"Thank you, Constance," Betty Ann said. "I think this is one of my better efforts."

Betty Ann had known Constance Baker for ten years. First, employed by Betty Ann's mother, Gaynell Moretta, and then, for the last six years, working with her in her own household. She always saw Constance as a "straight shooter," a person who possessed a tell-it-like-it-is approach to things. That was one of the reasons she liked her so much. Betty Ann had found, through the years, that Constance had become not only the housekeeper, but a confident, companion, and a very good friend.

Mrs. Baker went about putting the groceries away and Betty Ann poured herself another cup of coffee. When Mrs. Baker had finished in the kitchen, she took another pass by the flowers and shook her head.

"Amazing," she said. "It's just remarkable the things you can do, when you put your mind to it."

She then went over, leaned down, and kissed Betty Ann on the cheek. "You're capable of doing whatever you want to do," she said, "and I do mean whatever you want to do, Betty Ann."

Betty Ann knew exactly what she was referring to and that, in her own way, Constance had just given her approval and support for what was pending with Bob.

The serenity and blissfulness of the morning was interrupted by a brief stirring from the den. Betty Ann recognized the source of the noise, and grimaced slightly. It was her husband, Bob MacDonald, who was on the couch in a slothful slumber.

MacDonald, trying to overcome his previous evening's drunk, was oblivious to Betty Ann's presence. His presence, however, quickly reminded her of the realities of her life that the coming day was going to bring, both good and bad.

For the last year, she had let Bob's sounds cast dark shadows on her moods, but no longer. She knew that, in a few short hours, those days would be over and the heartaches she had suffered on an almost daily basis, since she had first married, were about to become a part of her past. She knew, if Bob were true to form, he would sleep until noon, remaining oblivious to the events about him for several more hours.

As the bacon began to crisp and the eggs started to scramble, she heard another sound. This time, however, it was a more gentle noise—one she looked forward to hearing every morning. Betty Ann looked up to see her six-year-old son, hair astray and his sister in tow, emerging from his upstairs bedroom. She watched with great joy as he diligently made his way down the stairway, carefully placing his tiny feet on each step as he descended.

Upon reaching the downstairs, the boy smiled. He paused for a second, wiped the sleep from his eyes, stretched a big stretch, and then let out a huge sigh, before he ran to his mother.

"Mommy," he asked, "what's for breakfast?"

Betty Ann laughed aloud and cheerfully embraced her child.

About an hour after breakfast, Betty Ann took the children out to the pool for a morning swim. How ironic it is, she thought, watching the child splash about in the water, that the secrets of life can usually be discovered by watching the innocent play of a child. Betty Ann wondered why adults always seem to forget how to derive pleasure from the elementary things in life. When do money, power, and all the other materialistic things overtake our common sense? Where is it all lost?

She reflected on her own childhood, remembering the time when her family was penniless. Her father had just died, the Depression was in full swing, and they lived in an old home in Lawndale, California, with her aunt and two cousins. It was a time when four children had shared the same bed, eaten lima bean soup for dinner every night, and each had one set of clothes to wear. Yet, while the family had struggled financially, it had been one of the best times of her life.

Betty Ann joyfully recalled the long evenings of playing hide-and-seek, kick-the-can, and freeze tag. She thought for a second, wondering when was the last time she'd shouted, at the top of her lungs, "Ollie, Ollie, Oxen free?!"

She remembered spending her days lying in a grassy field with her cousin, Marion, talking about daydreams, love, and always being happy. She took to heart the delights she'd found in walking along the beach and watching the waves crash along the shore, or how easy it had been to appreciate the dynamic beauty of each unique sunset, and how much warmth the flares of a beach bonfire could bring.

For Betty Ann, her youth had been a time when friendships were developed as a result of a person's character, instead of the clothes they wore, the type of car they drove, or what part of town they were from. She was disappointed with herself that she had been swayed away from those principles and joys, but now also took pride in having finally found the strength to rediscover the road to her personal happiness. She couldn't wait to start her journey back and share those things with her own children.

Her thoughts of the morning solidified in her belief that money couldn't assure euphoria, nor could it solve a person's problems. Her relationship with Bob was a testament to that. Better times were ahead, and that gave her the hope she needed to be strong.

An hour or so passed before Mrs. Baker called from the back door, "Betty Ann! Your mother is on the phone!"

Betty Ann immediately got to her feet. This was the call she had been anticipating. She took a deep breath, and said to herself, "The last hurdle to clear."

"Mother," Betty Ann said, with strong conviction in her voice, "I'm going through with my plans to leave Bob. I'm telling him today our marriage is over and he needs to leave!"

Gaynell had always fought her daughter's desire to divorce MacDonald. After all, Bob MacDonald was everything she'd wanted in a son-in-law. He was good-looking, rich, and his family ties to the Howard Hughes Empire gave the MacDonald name incredible social standing. She'd always considered Bob MacDonald a dream come true—not necessarily for her daughter, but certainly for her.

Betty Ann knew that, while her mother invariably understood her plight, she always seemed to find some obscure reason why her marriage to Bob needed to work. Be it financially related, socially related, or whatever, Gaynell's constant barrage of excuses for MacDonald's behavior was probably the only thing that had kept Betty Ann in the marriage for this long.

"In matters of divorce," Gaynell would say, "significant thought and consideration must be given and all possible ramifications should be explored, before such a life-changing decision is implemented."

This time, Betty Ann was prepared to stand firm in her resolve. She'd always thought Gaynell's ideas with regard to marriage were such "bullshit"! But until now, she'd never had the strength to defy her mother's constant pleas for her to stay with MacDonald.

Today, there would be no more excuses, no more pleas, no more hesitations. She knew what needed to be done, and was geared up for the ensuing war of words. Betty Ann was prepared. Her ammunition in place, she was ready to do battle.

But something strange happened. Gaynell was quiet. She hadn't said a single word in response to Betty Ann's announcement.

"Did you hear me, Mother?" Betty Ann asked. "I said, I'm telling Bob I want a divorce!"

Again, only absolute quiet. For a moment, Betty Ann thought she had lost the phone connection.

"For too many years," Gaynell said, breaking the silence, "I've made my priorities your priorities. With everything that's happened in the last few months, it's time I start making your priorities my priorities."

Betty Ann was stunned into silence. Having expected to become engaged in perhaps the most heated of their mother-daughter confrontations, she did not know how to respond to her mother's statement.

Gaynell, now crying, went on, "I've finally come to the conclusion," she said, "that what I've wanted or needed from life isn't necessarily what you want or what you need."

It was the MacDonald family's affluence, power, and social clout that had always clouded her better judgment in regard to Betty Ann and Bob. Gaynell, having been driven all her life by her greed for power, affluence, and social status, admittedly had always been willing to overlook her son-in-law's flaws. The fact that Bob was from a family with that type of influence and wealth had made her more tolerant of his behavior than she should have been. But clearly, the dramatic events of the previous few months had brought Gaynell to her senses. She knew it was time for her daughter to get out of the marriage, and she was finally supporting her decision to end it.

With her tone laced with strong conviction, Gaynell said to Betty Ann, "This time, I promise I'll be here for you!"

Betty Ann began to weep. After all the years of battling, bickering, and arguing with her mother about the horrors of her marriage, the fight was finally over. A monumental feeling of happiness rushed over her.

As she went to hang up the phone, she said, "Mom...thanks. I love you lots!"

Gaynell responded tearfully, "You're welcome, honey. I should have supported you like this a long time ago. I love you, too."

Gaynell got off the phone, feeling a tremendous amount of self-satisfaction. She knew she had finally done the right thing, and by doing so, had found a certain tranquility in finally having been able to unearth the courage necessary to support her daughter. For the first time in a long while, she felt good about herself.

Around noon, Betty Ann and her son prepared to leave the house for a dental appointment. As she left, Betty Ann was relieved that she did not have to talk to Bob, who, true to form, was still asleep on the couch. Her disdain for her husband had progressed to the point where even general conversations with him were unpleasant. She had developed a philosophy for dealing with him: Whenever contact can be avoided, avoid it.

Once outside, however, Betty Ann discovered that Bob's car was parked directly behind hers, blocking her way out of the driveway.

"Shit," she said, as she realized she had to return to the house. "Wait here," she said to her son. "Mommy is just going to get Daddy's car keys."

She put her son in the car and returned to the house. Looking for the keys, she entered the den. There, Betty Ann saw her husband snuggled in a blanket, in the fetal position. Despite the fact that she had grown to despise the man over the previous few months, she still felt an awkward sort of compassion for him as she looked down upon him. How could things have gone the way they did? she thought. How could they have become so horrible?

Betty Ann couldn't help but feel a Titanic sort of pity for her husband, as she acknowledged to herself that his life was on a collision course with disaster. No one could help him. She shook her head sadly, then resumed her search for the keys.

A strange, uncomfortable feeling came over her. Glancing back at Bob, she noticed that he was awake and staring at her with a sharp, piercing glare.

"I can't believe you're going to do this to me," he said in a grumble.

Betty Ann realized that he had obviously overheard her discussion with her mother.

"So," Bob continued, "you think you're fucking kicking me out of my own home? Bullshit!"

Not wanting a confrontation right then, Betty Ann responded, "Bob, please. I'm in a hurry. I need to get our son to his dentist appointment. I just want the keys to your car, so I can move it and go."

Bob ignored her plea. "If you think for one second," he screamed, "that you can get away with this, you're fucking crazy!"

Betty Ann listened to Bob's verbal tirade for as long as she could tolerate. "Shut the hell up," she said, "and give me the god-damn keys to your car so that I can go."

Bob's face flushed with anger. Betty Ann sensed that she had pushed the wrong button.

"Bob," she said, as calmly as possible, "I need to take our son to the dentist. Could I please have the keys to your car, so I can move it and be on my way?"

"I'm going to pack some things," Bob screamed, as he stormed up the stairs. "The keys to the car are upstairs! If you want 'em, you can fuckin' come up and get 'em!"

He disappeared into the bedroom. Betty Ann knew if she didn't accommodate Bob's request, she would miss a very-hard-to-get Saturday dentist appointment. She headed for the stairway.

Once at the top of the landing, Betty Ann looked down at Mrs. Baker, standing at the foot of the stairs. "Well," she said, "hopefully this will be the last time I have to do this."

Constance watched Betty Ann vanish into the upstairs bedroom. As soon as Betty Ann entered the room, Bob's verbal attack began, again. Sounds of his rage could be heard throughout the house.

Constance Baker had heard the sounds of Bob MacDonald's violence all too many times before. But as the argument upstairs increased, she quickly realized something was different. While Bob had initially been the aggressor in this battle, it was now Betty Ann who seemed to be on the offensive. Betty Ann was fighting back. After all the years of letting her husband verbally, physically, and emotionally abuse her, she was fighting back like a championship prizefighter.

"I'm done putting up with your shit," she screamed. "You're done hurting me! Do you understand that? You're done!"

Betty Ann continued as the verbal aggressor, screaming, "Where are the damn keys, Bob?"

When Bob failed to respond, she angrily repeated the question. "Where are the damn keys?" Betty Ann yelled. "I don't have time for this. Give me the fucking keys, now!"

For a fleeting moment, Mrs. Baker thought Betty Ann had finally been able to put Bob in his place. The strength of the young woman's refusal to be a party to any of her husband's further abuse caused an uneasy silence to fall over the entire house. But the situation soon changed.

"If you try to leave me," Bob yelled, breaking the quiet, "I'll kill you."

A cold chill ran through Mrs. Baker's body. Bob seemed to say those words with such conviction.

"I've put bullets into one of the most powerful men in the world," he screamed, "and I won't hesitate to do the same to you. Do you understand that, you fucking bitch?"

Constance knew Betty Ann was in serious trouble. Frantically trying to figure out what to do to defuse this frightful situation, her panic increased tenfold when she saw the MacDonald child had returned to the house and was making his way up the stairs.

As the boy reached the top step, Mrs. Baker saw him stop and stare into his parents' room. The sounds now coming from the room made it obvious that the confrontation between Bob and Betty

Ann had turned physically violent. Mrs. Baker began to make her way upstairs.

The MacDonald boy reached the door of the bedroom just as a shot rang out. Mrs. Baker froze. While a million horrible thoughts ran through her mind, during that split second, it was only when she heard Betty Ann cry out, "Please, dear God, no," that her worst fear was confirmed. Betty Ann had been shot.

Mrs. Baker hurried up the stairs. When she reached the halfway point, she saw the MacDonald child come hurtling out of the bedroom door, as if thrown by some incredible force. As the boy slammed against the banister railing, Betty Ann appeared in the bedroom doorway. Her upper body was soaked by an enormous amount of blood, but she managed to crawl out of the bedroom just in time to see Constance approaching. Betty Ann extended her hand toward Constance, shook her head no, then shifted her eyes toward her son.

"Oh, Mrs. Baker," she gasped.

Constance knew what Betty Ann wanted. She ran to the child, gathered him up in one fell swoop, and then ran toward the stairs. As she headed down, she glanced back at Betty Ann. For a brief moment, Betty Ann MacDonald's trademark smile appeared again on her face. She blinked the tears from her eyes and mouthed to her son, I love you!

A second shot rang out. A stream of blood viciously sprayed across the hallway, splattering against the far wall. Betty Ann lay face-down in a rapidly-growing puddle of blood.

The boy broke away from Mrs. Baker, and ran toward the bedroom door. With his mother dead near his feet, the MacDonald child locked a stunned gaze inside the room at his father.

Mrs. Baker heard Bob MacDonald's sobbing voice from inside the room, saying over and over again, "I'm sorry. I'm so sorry."

For a few seconds, there was an eerie silence. Then, the boy screamed, "No, Daddy! No!"

Another gunshot. Bob MacDonald had pulled the trigger one final time.

As Mrs. Baker approached the MacDonalds' bedroom, her primary concern was now for the safety of the child. Upon reaching the child, she embraced him, and held him as tightly and as close to her body as possible. She took him downstairs. Trying to calm him, she let the boy rock back and forth in her arms for several minutes.

The boy began to relax somewhat, his rocking slowed, and then finally stopped altogether. He looked up at Mrs. Baker and, with tears in his eyes, said, "My daddy went pow, pow, and then his head was gone."

Several minutes elapsed before Mrs. Baker let go of the boy. She made calls to Gaynell, Angus MacDonald, and then to the police—in that order. Although it was against her better judgment to do so, and dreading what she would find in the bedroom, she returned upstairs.

Dead, lying face-down near the door, was Betty Ann. She had been shot twice—once in the back and once through her head. The once-small puddle of blood had now grown into a large pool, staining the white-carpeted floor upon which she lay.

Mrs. Baker looked at the dead woman, overcome by the irony of the day. How could the vividness and spectacular contrast of the colors red and white, which fewer than four hours earlier had been so eloquently fashioned into an exquisite rose floral arrangement by Betty Ann, possibly be the same colors that now defined the grim reality of her hideous death? Constance burst into tears.

Somewhat regaining her composure, she continued to look about the room. Bob MacDonald's lifeless body was sprawled across the floor next to the bed. His head was all but gone.

By placing the barrel of a .30-caliber carbine rifle in his mouth and pulling the trigger, he had apparently found the solution to all the problems he had created for himself.

The horror of the scene finally overtook Constance Baker. Legs shaking, hands trembling, and her stomach wrenching with nausea, she slid to the floor and again began to cry—this time, uncontrollably.

As news of the MacDonald murder/suicide spread through the high society world of which they were constituents, a shocked community asked, "Why? Why and how could such a thing happen?"

The next day, the MacDonald murder/suicide was front-page news. The Los Angeles Times ran the story, complete with pictures of Bob and Betty Ann, with the caption "Man Kills Wealthy Wife and Ends Life with Gun."

Immediately after this tragic event and the initial reporting of it, a shroud of secrecy was thrown over the entire situation. Almost overnight, it appeared as if no one wanted to know why Bob Mac-Donald, aged twenty-seven, the son of a millionaire, World War II hero, the winner of three Purple Hearts, a Bronze Star, a Silver Star, and the father of two, had taken a .30-caliber, army-type, carbine rifle and murdered his wife, then put the muzzle of the weapon in his mouth and taken his own life.

The press had their first front-page murder story since the killing of the famous gangster, Benjamin "Bugsy" Siegel, which had taken place some three months before. While this murder may not have been of the same infamous stature as the Siegel killing, surely the fact that the MacDonalds were tied to Howard Hughes, Gaynell had been associated with Los Angeles city politics, and Bob and Betty Ann were from the Southern California aristocratic society where this type of thing "just doesn't happen," made the story newsworthy. But the press, strangely, only ran one other article on the killing, a short blurb that stated that Betty Ann's mother, Gaynell, was to obtain temporary custody of the MacDonald children. Today, an event like the MacDonald slaying would be on every television talk show and in every supermarket tabloid across the country.

The police investigating the MacDonald case stated the reasons behind Bob MacDonald's gruesome act were simply unexplainable. The case was closed after just three days. Even the families of the victims publicly stated they were baffled by MacDonald's bizarre behavior and had no information that would help provide any insight into what could have driven him to such madness. They were not being truthful. Ironically, the impetus that led Bob MacDonald to commit his hideous act would be the same reason the two family patriarchs believed they had to form a consortium of secrecy, to protect their own wealth, political power, and elite social status from the dark secret that had led MacDonald down his path of destruction.

"Achieving the things you want in life means nothing," Angus MacDonald, Bob's father, had once said. "It only matters that, once you get what you want, you have the ability to do whatever it takes to keep it. We all have skeletons in our closets; some of us have more than others. That's just life. We all have secrets we want to keep from the rest of the world."

When this particular skeleton was placed in our family closet, it was done so for the express purpose of hiding from the rest of the world the astonishing true facts behind our...Family Secret.

Chapter Two
The Journey Begins

Thanksgiving 1996

As a result of my being a football coach, my wife Annette and I have lived a fairly nomadic lifestyle. We have moved around the country, to various states, working our way through the coaching circuit. In 1996, I was coaching football at Sonoma State University in Rohnert Park, California—a community just north of San Francisco—while Annette was managing a Starbuck's Coffee shop in San Rafael.

No matter where Annette and I lived, we usually tried to spend either Thanksgiving or Christmas with our families who lived in Southern California. That year, however, our work responsibilities dictated that we remain in Northern California for Thanksgiving.

Annette and I shared a private Thanksgiving Day and then chatted on the phone with our families. After talking with Annette's mother, Maaike, we called my home. Everyone seemed to be in high spirits, especially my father. Dad's birthday sometimes fell on Thanksgiving, and as it happened, that year my father was celebrating his seventy-seventh.

Dad was concerned about the typical things. He wanted to know how we were doing, asked me to explain a few calls made by several football coaches whose teams had played—and lost—that day, and was very excited about our upcoming Christmas visit. My father was somewhat hard of hearing, so spending a great deal of time on the phone was not a common occurrence. Yet, on that night, he seemed exceptionally chatty.

After about twenty minutes talking on the phone, Annette and I wrapped up the conversation by assuring Dad we would be down for Christmas.

* * * * *

At about 3:00 A.M., the phone rang. I groggily reached for the receiver.

"Hello," I muttered in a raspy voice.

"Hey! It's me."

I vaguely recognized the voice as my brother Rick's. "What's wrong?" I asked.

"First of all, Dad's doing okay," my brother said. "But he's had a stroke. Can you and Annette get down here? The sooner, the better!"

"What?" I said, sitting up in bed. "Say that again."

"Dad's had a stroke," my brother repeated. "When can you leave?"

"We'll leave now," I muttered.

Within a matter of minutes, Annette and I were dressed, packed, had our dog, Knute, in the car, and were on the road. While Annette and I tried to engage in some idle chitchat during the 450-mile ride, we were both lost in our independent thoughts.

I felt a sickness, unlike anything I had ever felt before. My mind raced with thousands of questions. Was my father still alive? If so, what type of condition was he going to be in? What were the worst-case scenarios with a stroke victim? What was the best?

I sadly wondered if my Thanksgiving Day chat with my father was to be the last coherent conversation I was going to experience with him.

The drive seemed to take an eternity, but eventually, we arrived at the hospital. I looked at my watch. It was eleven o'clock in the morning.

Eight hours in the car, combined with a half-dozen cheap cups of coffee, produced a horrible feeling. So, as I stepped out of the car, I took a deep breath. The air was cold but felt cleansing. My head began to clear and I thought I was ready to face the task at hand.

Approaching the front door of the hospital, I suddenly began to feel sick again. I realized I wasn't as ready as I'd thought. My mind flooded with horrible thoughts; I prayed that my father was still alive.

Annette headed straight for the information desk. I hesitated at the front door for a moment and then detoured toward the water fountain. I had a drink of water; splashed my face three or four times, stood tall, and took another deep, gathering breath.

I still felt like shit!

Annette returned to my side, and waited patiently as I went through the same cycle again and again; drink, splash, breath. Annette knew every avoidance tactic I had in my bag of tricks. She understood that my diversion to the drinking fountain wasn't to satisfy my thirst, but was my way of preparing myself for what lay ahead.

"Dad's in 303," she said.

While I wanted to move, my body refused to obey. I merely stood there, waiting for something to happen. Nothing did.

I looked about the hospital. I hated what I saw. Probably a more accurate statement would be, I hated why I was there. I thought to myself, *God, I love my father; please don't take him from us. There are too many things left for us to do.* I began to cry.

Annette engulfed me in a hug and just held me. The knot in my stomach had climbed into my throat, not allowing me to speak, so I just held my wife tightly for a few moments, until I finally gathered myself.

"Thanks," I said in a hushed voice. "I'm fine."

Annette knew better, but she gathered my hand in hers, and she led me down the hallway, around the corner, and to the elevator door. The two-floor journey seemed to take an eternity, but it did provide me with ample time to bitch about everything and anything I could. I complained about the drive, the cold air outside, being back in the town where I had grown up, and probably the price of tea in China. Annette just let me go.

The doors finally opened, and the strong smell of antiseptic wash filled my nostrils. "I hate that smell," I said, as I exited the elevator.

"Okay," Annette said. "You're done!"

I knew what she was talking about, and she was right. It was time for me to be positive and face the task at hand.

I spotted my brother standing in the hall. His head was down, and he was shaking his head. My heart sank.

As we got closer, however, I noticed my brother lift his head and let out a chuckle. Then, as we neared my father's room, I heard something that washed away all of my anxiety…laughter. When my brother saw us coming, he produced a beaming smile and greeted us excitedly.

"You guys made it," he exclaimed. "Dad's doing great."

Gazing into the room, I saw my father sitting up in his bed, recovering from a chuckle. Forget the fact that he was on oxygen and that miles of intravenous lines connected him to several monitors, the sight of seeing him engaged in a laugh produced the most incredible feeling.

With several nurses gathered by his bed, Dad was in his storytelling mode. He could spin a yarn with the best of them. His stories were told from the heart and with such tremendous enthusiasm that, if you shut your eyes and listened, the images came to life in your mind. Seeing him doing what he liked to do best eased my mind and warmed my heart.

Both Annette and I gave a sigh of relief. My chest pain instantly subsided, the knot in my stomach eased, and I felt as if my emotions had been given a stay of execution.

When my father looked up and saw Annette and me by the doorway, I could see the joy in his eyes. Annette approached him. Dad smiled widely and greeted her by lifting his right arm. When she reached his side, he engulfed her in a bear-like hug—a wonderful sight.

Annette and my father had developed a unique bond over the years. She was the little girl my father could love, spoil, and at times, bicker with over trivial things. Dad was the kind, fatherly figure Annette had never had—a gentle man who never mocked her dreams and accepted her for who and what she was—a woman of strong will and silent determination. Annette also possesses a marvelous sense of humor and a spunky attitude, which were two of the qualities my father admired most in her. He liked the fact that my wife was a smart ass.

After Annette and Dad broke their embrace, he lay back upon the bed. There were tears in his eyes, which he quickly wiped away and replaced with a soft smile.

My father looked at me and assumed his favorite guise, that of a gruff old man. It was a pretext that never suited him, nor was it a role he could portray very well.

"What the hell did you kids drive all the way down here for?" Dad barked. "Ya got better things to do with your time than drive all the way down here, don't ya?"

"Nope," I said, approaching the bed. "We sure don't." I bent over and kissed my father, still shaking with joy. "You scared the shit out of me," I said in a whisper.

"Think you were scared?" he snickered. "Just think how I felt after they told me if I couldn't pee and they were going to have to catheterize me."

My father had made me laugh. I felt better.

My mother entered the room. She had been talking to the doctors, but she failed to allow the seriousness of what they told her to blemish the lightheartedness of the moment. She hugged both Annette and me.

"Told you they'd get here in a hurry," she said to Dad.

* * * * *

For the next several hours, it was Dad's show. Whatever he wanted was what he was going to get, and what Dad wanted was to tell stories...so he did.

Listening to my father tell tales had always been a way of life for me. There were some stories he told over and over, while others made only one appearance and were never heard again. As we went through the remainder of the day, we heard several of his favorites. As usual, with all of Dad's tales, we smiled, we laughed, we cried, and we learned a lesson or two about life.

At about six o'clock, a nurse wheeled in a supper cart, pulled my father's meal from the hot box, and placed it in front of him. My father smiled politely at the nurse, then waited for her to leave, before he looked at the tray, grunted in disgust, and then continued with his story.

By that time, I was starving, so much so that even the grotesque offering of neatly-packaged, compartmented food looked like a gourmet meal. My stomach growled.

"Maybe you should all go grab a bite to eat," Dad said.

"No way," I snapped back. "We didn't come all the way down here to go out to dinner. We'll get something when we leave."

While dinner at Claim Jumper's Restaurant would have been nice, all I wanted was to keep hearing my father's voice. I just wanted to listen to him laugh and see him smile. I just wanted him to keep going and going and going. Everyone else shared my thoughts, so we all listened to Dad for a few more hours. It was wonderful.

At about nine o'clock, the nurse came into the room. "I'm sorry," she said. "Visiting hours ended at eight. I have to ask you all to leave."

No one really wanted to leave, but common sense and hunger pains had gotten the best of us all. As Annette, my brother, and my mother said their farewells and I studied my father. He was a tired man, not just because of the stroke, or from the verbal activity of the evening, but from life.

My father had seen a great deal in his day. A World War II veteran, he was among the first U.S. soldiers to arrive at the German death camp of Auschwitz. He only told one story of the horrors of that experience. I knew the nightmares of seeing the bodies of human beings smoldering in the death ovens had taken their toll on him through the years. He had seen the worst life had to offer; fortunately, he had also seen the best.

When I leaned over and gave my father a kiss, I noticed his eyes were filled with sadness. Despite my search, the characteristic Cheshire-cat smile he always sported was nowhere to be found. *Oh shit*, I thought. *Here come the tears.*

I was supposed to be the strong one. At 6-feet 2-inches, 230 pounds, my shoulders were the broadest in the family. As a college football player, college football coach, and former member of the National Security Agency, I was the tough guy. It had always been my responsibility not to crack, not to show my emotions, and to always be the pillar of strength in a situation like this. What a crock of shit! I was crying, and only my father could see my tears.

His expression warmed, which caused my tears to flow harder. He gathered one of my hands into his and caressed it softly. His much-appreciated attempt at comforting me caused his intravenous lines to become tangled on the bed rails. As he attempted to free himself, things only got worse, and within seconds, the plastic tubes had transformed themselves into an evil creature from a horror movie, wrapping around whatever moved and made for a very comical sight.

"Damn things," Dad giggled, as he attempted to get free from the rubberized monster.

A million thoughts raced through my mind, but one stuck out: I was fortunate to have this man as my father. Even in the worst of times, his wonderful sense of humor stayed intact. A frustrating situation was defused with a simple dash of his wit.

After Dad got untangled, he smiled. Then, his expression became somewhat serious.

"I need to talk to you alone, for a while, Boo," he said. "Have everyone go on, so that we can chat."

My father had only called me "Boo" on three occasions in my life. The first time was when my grandmother had died. The second time was when my Saint Bernard dog had died. And the third time was when he'd backed over my motorcycle with his truck. I was hoping this wasn't going to be another conversation about death and destruction.

"I'm staying here," I exclaimed. "Dad and I need to visit a while longer."

My family gave no argument. After another round of good-byes, my brother made a bee-line out the door. He was exhausted. He'd been at the hospital since 3:00 A.M. but had been up since 5:00 A.M. the previous day. Thirty-seven hours was about his limit.

Annette kiseed me. "This will be good for you," she said. "You and Dad need some time together." She kissed me again, kissed Dad again, and then exited the room with my brother.

Dad looked at my mother. "I'm going to tell him everything," he said.

My mother went back to my father's side and began to caress his face with the back of her hand tenderly. My parents had been married fifty-three years, and I had seldom seen them show much affection toward each other. Yet, in that single moment, I could see the love they had shared reflected in their gaze. It was awesome!

Mom bent over and kissed Dad on the cheek. As she did, he whispered something to her, which caused her to chuckle.

"What's going on?" I asked.

My mother and father shared another kiss, and then Mom broke from Dad and walked to where I was standing. "Your father has some things he thinks you should know," she said. "I agree with him."

"What things?" I asked.

"Things we should have told you years ago."

"So, are you going to tell me I'm adopted?" I said, only half-jokingly.

"This isn't going to be quite that simple," she said with a chortle. "I love you, Boo."

Mom left the room, met Annette in the hall, and walked with her down the corridor. I turned my attention to my father.

"What's that mean?" I asked.

"Here," he said, pushing his food tray toward me. "I know you're hungry. Help yourself."

I looked at the tray. "No, thanks. I'm not that hungry."

I pulled the green, plastic-covered hospital chair up beside my father and plopped down. "Okay," I said, "what's the big secret?"

Dad reached over and grabbed my arm. "There are some things that your mother and I should have shared with you a long time ago," he said. "Things you need to know about, and maybe, just maybe, do something about."

There was a pensive silence. He took a few sips from a plastic cup of water. I wondered what in the world my father had to tell me that was creating this type of hesitation on his part. My father had always been an honest man. He worked hard, provided for his family, treated people with respect and dignity, and lived his life in a way that he, his wife, and his children were all able to take a great deal of pride in. What could he possibly have to say that was making him so nervous?

Dad gestured toward the nightstand next to his bed. "Open the top drawer," he said.

I pulled open the drawer and saw a medium-sized cedar box. The box had an elegantly engraved rose decorating the lid. It looked fairly old. Almost immediately after I had the box in my hands, Dad reached for it, like a child trying to get their hands on a gift at Christmas.

"Everything you need to know to tell the story is in here," he said, as he tapped the box with his hand. "The only way for a person to be able to solve a puzzle is to start with all the pieces. Your mother and I are the only ones left who have all the pieces to the puzzle. We have a secret no one else knows."

"A secret?" I asked. "What kind of secret?"

Dad scooted up on the pillows of his bed, and he opened the box. "It's all here," he said. "Everything you need to get started. Everything you need to have, so you can fully understand our little family secret."

"What fucking secret?"

My father smiled again and then began pulling a number of old newspaper clippings and photographs from the cedar box. I watched him intently, as he shuffled through the items and started placing the articles and photographs in a sequential order upon his bed. He took a long look at a tattered, torn, and yellowed newspaper clipping, then, hands trembling, he handed it to me.

"I wish my shakiness were because of the stroke," he said.

I looked at the article. The headline read, "Man Kills Wealthy Wife and Ends Life with Gun—West End Home Tragedy Follows Making of Will by Woman Leaving $100,000.00 to Their Children." I had very vague memories of Betty Ann Rockwell. I knew she was my mother's cousin, I knew she was my mother's best friend, and I knew Betty Ann had been murdered by her husband.

Betty Ann's picture accompanied the article. I had never seen a photograph of her before. Although I was looking at a fifty-year-old newspaper clipping, her image instantly captured me. What I first noticed about her were her eyes; they were soulful...loving.

"Betty Ann's death was on the front page of every paper in Los Angeles," my father said. "The article you have in your hand is from the *Los Angeles Times.*"

"This picture was on the front page of the *Los Angeles Times?*" I asked.

"Yep! September 14, 1947."

My mind began racing. "Where is this going?" I asked.

"Read the clipping first, Boo," he said.

I shifted my attention to the article.

"Gunfire and death yesterday ended a marriage which began with an elopement in 1940, when former Lt. Robert MacDonald, 27, killed his pretty wife, Betty Ann Rockwell MacDonald, 24, graduate of an exclusive girls' school, and then took his own life. The shooting occurred at the couple's home, 822 Warner Ave., West Los Angeles.

"The tragedy followed by a few hours Mrs. MacDonald's action in executing a will, leaving her estate, estimated at $100,000.00, to the couple's two children.

"Her attorney, Birger Tinglof, told police that Mrs. Mac-Donald called him Friday night and insisted that a will be drawn up immediately. Tinglof said that Mrs. MacDonald declared she was without fear, although police were told her husband had threatened her on previous occasions.

"Husband Under Treatment.

"MacDonald, who fought in the European Theater and won three Purple Hearts, the Silver Star, and the Bronze Star, was reported to have been receiving psychiatric treatment at the Veterans Facility at Sawtelle.

"The family trouble had been punctuated by a divorce action filed by Mrs. MacDonald about five months ago, and then withdrawn. It was reported that she again was taking steps to sue for divorce.

"Police were told the husband had slept in the den of their attractive home on Friday night, and awakened shortly before noon when Mrs. MacDonald asked him to move his car from the drive so she could drive their son to the dentist.

"Argument Reported!

"Instead, police said, he asked her to accompany him to an upstairs bedroom. From the room came sounds of scuffling, then loud voices, Mrs. Constance Baker, the children's nurse, told police. She said she ran upstairs and, as she neared the upper landing, the boy came hurtling out of the bedroom door, as if thrown, and then she heard shots.

"MacDonald shot his wife once in the chest and once in the head with an army-type carbine, taken from a sizable collection of war weapons he kept at the home. He then placed the muzzle in his mouth and killed himself.

"The will which was executed Friday night named Mrs. MacDonald's mother, Mrs. Gaynell Moretta, of 9644 Olympic Blvd., as executrix of the will and guardian of the children. Mrs. Moretta told police that MacDonald enlisted shortly after Pearl Harbor. She said that he had not had a regular job since his discharge in 1945, and that she believed some of the couple's trouble grew out of the wife's insistence that he obtain employment."

I finished reading the story and looked at my father. "Okay," I asked again, "where's this going?"

"You would have liked Betty Ann," he said, ignoring my question but extending his hand to retrieve the article. "You would have liked her a lot. If she had lived, she would have liked you, too."

I handed my father back the clipping. He studied Betty Ann's picture, the sadness in his heart evident.

"Boo," he declared softly, "there's more to Betty Ann's death than you know. Hell, there's more to Betty Ann's death than anyone knows.

"Your mother and I decided we want you to know the truth. We want you to know everything. "You have to promise me you'll find a way to tell the world what I'm going to share with you!"

"Tell the world?" I said. "Tell the world what?"

Dad grinned, then handed me another newspaper clipping. "By the time we're done, you'll know why it happened, why it was kept a secret, and why the world never discovered the truth."

I saw the headline of the article in my hand, and everything came together. "Are you kidding me?" I said, keeping my eyes on the newspaper article. "Those stories were all true?"

I read the headlines: "Someone Knows! Bugsy Siegel's Killer Went at His Work With Placid, Unhurried Craftsmanship."

"Are you serious?" I asked.

"I'm afraid so, Boo," he said.

The article, written by Herb Stinson of *The Mirror*, a Los Angeles magazine publication, was in regards to the mystery surrounding the internationally famous killing of one of America's most notorious gangsters, Bugsy Siegel.

"If anyone had discovered the answer to that reporter's question," Dad said, "all hell would have broken loose; at least from the family's standpoint."

The characteristic Cheshire-cat smile I had lost all hope of ever seeing again reappeared on his face. "I'm going to tell you one of the most amazing stories you've ever heard. I'm going to share with you the family secret."

Over the next few hours, my father shuffled through the items he had skillfully placed upon his bed and removed the shroud of secrecy, which had skillfully cloaked the skeleton in our family closet for almost fifty years. After he had completed telling me this incredible tale, I was sure of one thing: While Dad had shared many stories with me during his time on earth, apparently he had chosen to save the most amazing tale for last.

On December 6, 1996, my father, Robert Hull passed away at the age of 77.

Chapter Three
The Early Rockwells

L orenzo Rockwell was born in Canada in 1850. At the age of fifteen, he left his family and moved to Richford, Vermont—a community known for its fertile farmland, textile plants, and need for men with strong wills and even stronger backs.

By 1875, Lorenzo had established himself as one of the finest brick masons in the Northeast. Considered a solid construction man with excellent skills and a tremendous work ethic, by the age of twenty-five, Lorenzo's professional career was moving in a good direction.

It was shortly thereafter that Lorenzo married a local woman named Betsy Carver. At first, it seemed as if Lorenzo was to live a full and happy life, but fate stepped in and provided a cruel twist.

A year after Betsy and Lorenzo were married, Betsy died giving birth to the couple's first child—a daughter named Claudia. Lorenzo was devastated by the loss of his wife. Sadly, Lorenzo's way of handling tragedy was to submerge himself in his work, leaving Claudia to be raised by friends and neighbors.

In the spring of 1885, the owners of the city's largest textile plant put their business up for sale. Lorenzo, who had been working sixteen-hour days for ten years, decided he was going to purchase the property and make a run at being a businessman. His attempt at becoming a merchandiser was a success, and within a few years, Lorenzo's textile plant was a prospering business.

In the fall of 1890, Lorenzo met Linnie Mills, a classmate of Claudia's, who was now fifteen years old. By Christmas of that same year, the forty-year-old Rockwell and the fourteen-year-old Linnie Mills had become husband and wife. It was a relationship that changed the direction of Lorenzo's life.

It was not long after Linnie and Lorenzo married that the two women in Rockwell's life were at each other's throats. Claudia never approved of the relationship her father had with her former friend. She maintained that attitude even after Linnie and Lorenzo were wed.

Linnie told her husband that Claudia's prejudices against her were making her feel too uncomfortable to be a good wife, and if Lorenzo wanted to have a proper marriage, he would have to send his daughter away. Lorenzo honored his bride's request, and Claudia was shipped off to live with her mother's family.

With Claudia gone, Lorenzo and Linnie began their life together. In 1892, Linnie gave birth to the couple's first child, Luvie. Seven more children followed: Ruben in 1894, Claude in 1896, Florence (Flossy) in 1898, Renny in 1900, Homer in 1902, Guy in 1904, and Mills in 1905. When Mills was born, Lorenzo was fifty-six years old.

While Linnie was giving birth to the Rockwell children, Lorenzo was expanding the family business opportunities. Lorenzo bought a 150-acre farm. As the farm had some of the best grazing in the state, Lorenzo also purchased a herd of dairy cows, which in turn, led to the development of a cheese factory.

By the start of 1905, the Rockwell family had two successful businesses in place, and by all accounts, Lorenzo Rockwell should have entered his old age in comfort and without financial worry. There was one problem, however—Linnie Rockwell!

In May of 1905, Claudia returned to Richford to introduce her three children to their grandfather. Deep down, Lorenzo had always regretted exiling his daughter. He had long come to believe he was wrong in doing what he had done, so initially, Lorenzo wanted to welcome Claudia and her children with open arms.

Linnie, however, wanted nothing to do with reuniting father and daughter, and viewed Claudia's return as an attempt by her to steal a piece of the Rockwell family fortune. A paranoid, greedy woman, Linnie came up with a scheme, which in her mind would protect the family fortune from Claudia. Linnie's plan was to take everything the family owned and transfer ownership to Homer Adams, a long-time friend of Lorenzo's who had been working with the Rockwells for almost a dozen years.

She was adamant about having Adams assume paper control over the Rockwell empire, assuring her husband they could trust him implicitly. After all, Adams and his wife had been friends of the family for a long time.

What Linnie did not declare, however, was that she and Homer Adams had been having an affair for the previous two years. Lorenzo Rockwell was simply a workaholic; not Linnie's idea of the perfect husband.

Linnie was the mother of eight children and twenty-nine years of age when she began her affair with Adams. She felt as if she was missing life, and wanted to start anew. Lorenzo was not in Linnie's plans. Gaining control of his money was.

Linnie and Adams had planned to run off together, so Claudia's arrival merely allowed Linnie and her lover to hatch a scheme to steal Lorenzo Rockwell's life's work. If Linnie could convince Lorenzo to sign over the family holdings to Adams, she and her lover would have complete control over the Rockwell assets. Linnie and Adams could then dump their respective spouses, sell the Rockwell properties, run off into the sunset together, and live happily ever after.

Lorenzo and Linnie went around and around on the matter for weeks, but eventually, Lorenzo agreed to sign the documents and give Homer Adams total control of the family possessions. In Linnie's eyes, the plan was flawless.

There was one problem, however. Two weeks after assuming ownership of the Rockwell holdings, Homer Adams, at the age of thirty-five, dropped dead from a massive heart attack. When Adams died, Mrs. Homer Adams became sole beneficiary of his property.

Upon the death of her husband, Mrs. Adams liquidated every asset in his name. She was fully aware of the affair her husband was having with Linnie, and by Christmas of 1905, a very wealthy Mrs. Adams moved from Vermont to Florida, where she lived happily ever after.

In a *Twilight Zone*-type moment, Linnie had indeed figured out the perfect way to screw Claudia out of receiving any Rockwell money. Unfortunately for the Rockwells, Linnie's brilliant plan ended up not only screwing Claudia but also the entire Rockwell family.

Linnie never revealed to Lorenzo her plans with Adams. That revelation came many years later, however, due to her greed. Linnie and

Lorenzo Rockwell were forced to reinvent their lives. They decided to do so by moving to California.

Lorenzo had an older brother named Timothy, who lived in San Francisco. For years, Timothy had tried to convince his brother to come to California. Timothy had ties to San Francisco's growing artistic community and just knew the Rockwells' oldest child, Luvie, could make a fortune with her artistic ability.

Timothy's perception of his niece had merit, as the very first painting Luvie ever did was that of an Indian on horseback. The painting hung in the Vermont State Museum. Later in life, Luvie painted a picture for Philip K. Wrigley, owner of the Chicago Cubs, namesake of Wrigley Field. The picture was of a horse named Khoorsheed, who according to Mr. Wrigley in a letter written to Luvie in 1958, "was a chestnut with a great deal of red in his coat. His color was on the dark side, but in the sunlight, he was almost a maroon color, reddish brown." Luvie captured Khoorsheed to perfection. Her ability as an artist was recognized, and Mr. Wrigley paid a handsome amount of money for her efforts.

Timothy offered to pay for Luvie's ticket west. Timothy knew Luvie could make money with her work. With few options, Lorenzo agreed to send his daughter to California ahead of the family. While the plan had merit, Luvie's trip to California turned out to be a horror story.

Toward the end of Luvie's journey, Mexican bandits raided the train and took Luvie captive. Officials were of little value in trying to help Lorenzo locate Luvie. How could they? The family was left to assume that Luvie had been taken into Mexico, used for whatever horrible purposes that met the needs of her kidnappers, and then murdered.

With the tragedy surrounding his oldest child, Lorenzo re-evaluated his plan and decided he would go to California ahead of his family. By working from sunup to sundown, he believed he could save enough money within a year to bring his entire family to California in one move.

As for Luvie Rockwell, while she had not been murdered, she had been sold by white slavers to a whorehouse in Mexico. Eventually, she escaped her life of slavery, after an American businessman, a frequent customer at the brothel, paid for her freedom. The man brought Luvie back to the United States, but she was not reunited with her family for several years.

Luvie's experience in Mexico left her a bitter, cold-hearted person, who seldom saw any good in people. In her later years, she asserted that she spent time with the notorious John Dillinger, a claim never disputed, especially when, as the records show, Luvie spent time in a Colorado federal prison for armed robbery, a crime she committed without Dillinger.

As for Lorenzo, he did go west and arrived in San Francisco on April 13, 1906. Two days later, on April 15th, the City on the Bay was hit by one of the most significant earthquakes in United States history. The earthquake, measuring 7.8 on the Richter scale, rocked San Francisco. It killed over seven hundred people, and financial losses to the city totaled more than four hundred million dollars.

From April of 1906 to June of 1907, the city of San Francisco came under the control of the State of California, and all occupants of the town were subject to martial law. As a new member of the 32nd Street Masons' Union, Lorenzo was enlisted to help rebuild the city of San Francisco. By law, he had to remain in the city, working for free, until the job was complete.

For the next fourteen months, Lorenzo was essentially a captive of the state. As a consequence, the Rockwell family, still living in Vermont, struggled to survive. During the winter of 1906, Linnie and the children were living in the basement of an old, burned-out house. The cold and the exposure to the elements caused Mills Rockwell, the youngest child, to become sick and die.

Out west, Lorenzo had to fight for his survival, as well. Even before the quake, San Francisco was an ill-tempered town. It wasn't uncommon for men to be taken into involuntary servitude by ships' scouts.

Ships' scouts were men who answered the needs of the shipping industry's staffing concerns. Scouts would find a man, liquor him up, knock him over the head, and then drag the unconscious man to a departing vessel. The unconscious man would be placed aboard the ship, and by the time he awoke from being clunked on the head, the ship was usually miles out to sea. With no other options but to serve aboard the vessel, the man was forced to work for the duration of his voyage. Lorenzo encountered such a situation, and only by a stroke of luck did he manage to survive the ordeal.

One evening, he was in a bar, in the company of several rather shady characters. After talking to the men for a short period of time, Lorenzo figured out his new friends were bad news. Lorenzo took his leave, exited the bar, and headed down the street toward his flophouse. After walking a few blocks, he was attacked by two of the men and knocked unconscious.

The men grabbed Lorenzo under his arms, hoisted him to his feet, and began to walk him through the city streets. The men pretended he was a drunken sailor friend they were returning to their ship. By all accounts, Lorenzo was headed for a life of servitude.

However, just as his kidnappers hit the pier, Lorenzo began to regain consciousness. As he groggily looked about, he saw a group of men standing along the wharf. Unable to form any words, he did the only thing he could think of; he flashed a hand signal, which was a distress sign for a man of the 32nd-degree Masons.

By a stroke of luck, the men were Masons. Having recognized Lorenzo's flash as a call for help, the men quickly figured out what was happening, and charged the men carrying Lorenzo. Lorenzo's captors dropped him and ran off.

From that point forward, Lorenzo never drank alone. In reflection, years later, he acknowledged that being a Mason was probably the only thing that saved his life that night.

Twenty-two months after his arrival in San Francisco, Lorenzo sent for his family, and the Rockwells were reunited in the winter of 1908. In the spring of 1909, the family moved to Southern California, where they made a new home in Los Angeles.

Lorenzo knew life was hard for the family, but they were together, and in his eyes, that was all that mattered. Linnie, however, had other perceptions. She saw Lorenzo, now in his mid-sixties, as an old, worn-out, tired man who was of very little use to her.

Even though Linnie's greed had put the family in the position they were in, she never did own up to her role in the demise of the family, nor did she ever accept responsibility for what had happened in Vermont. Instead, Linnie became involved with another man, and shortly thereafter, Lorenzo and Linnie separated, then divorced. When Linnie and Lorenzo went their separate ways, all but one of the Rockwell children stayed with their father.

Lorenzo focused his attention on providing for his family. To accomplish this, he returned to the skills he had learned while working as a brick mason in Vermont. Every day, Lorenzo loaded his wheelbarrow up with supplies and walked the streets of Los Angeles, looking for work. One day, he came across a man who was building a bakery, and after chatting with him for a few minutes, Lorenzo was offered a job. For the next few months, Lorenzo had steady employment, made a good wage, and started to get the family back on its feet.

Lorenzo had a tremendous work ethic, so much so that he was always the last to leave a work site. He made it a point to never leave a location without doing some type of landscaping or a little-added masonry work. This trait caught the eye of the owner of the bakery. The man was so impressed with Lorenzo's work that he began referring Rockwell to his friends. As it turned out, the man Lorenzo worked for was the founding father of Weber Bread and Baked Goods. Weber's company went on to become one of the largest bakeries in California, and with Mr. Weber recommending him for jobs, Lorenzo never had to seek out employment again.

For the rest of his life, every night, no matter where Lorenzo worked during the day, he always stopped by the bakery to visit with Mr. Weber. And every night, when their visit was concluded, Mr. Weber loaded Lorenzo's wheelbarrow with all kinds of baked goods. While Lorenzo never did regain his fortune, he did manage to live somewhat comfortably for the rest of his life, and his children never went hungry.

In 1931, a car being driven by a drunk driver struck Lorenzo, as he crossed the street. Lorenzo, who was pushing his wheelbarrow along Redondo Beach Boulevard, suffered a broken femur, a fractured arm, multiple abrasions, and contusions. Tragically, Lorenzo would succumb as a result of this ordeal—not as a result of his injuries sustained in the accident, but rather by the carelessness of a hospital orderly.

Lorenzo had been placed in a bathtub for his daily washing. The orderly began to draw the water when a nurse in the room across the hall gave a cry for help. When the orderly went to render assistance to his coworker, he left the water in Lorenzo's tub running, and as the water made its way through the pipes, it became hotter and hotter, to the point of being scalding.

The sounds of the emergency occurring across the hall apparently cloaked Lorenzo's screams for help. So when the orderly returned to Lorenzo, the Rockwell family patriarch had been scalded over ninety percent of his body. Lorenzo didn't have the strength to fight, and a few days later, passed away at the age of eighty-eight.

Chapter Four
Renny and Gaynell

January 1912

It was a rather typical winter day in Akron, Ohio—snow, bitter cold, and wind. Most everyone walking to the train station was cursing the elements. The lone exception was Frederick Wolfe.

Fredrick had lived in Ohio for much of his life, and knew the miseries offered by a Midwestern winter day. Despite the weather, this was a great day for Fredrick. He was placing his family on a train bound for sunny Southern California, and was going to join them a few days later. While Fredrick had initially planned on making the trip to Los Angeles with his wife, Percy, and daughter Gaynell, a last-minute snafu concerning the sale of their home had necessitated a postponement of his departure. Frederick saw no reason to delay the exodus of his family from their wintry prison. After all, he was probably only going to be two or three more days, so why rearrange everyone's travel plans?

As the Wolfe family made their way through the train station, Frederick looked at his daughter and chuckled. Gaynell was Frederick's pride and joy. Percy had done an excellent job of protecting Gaynell from the cold that morning, but being wrapped in a heavy winter jacket, gloves, two pants, and a fur hat meant Gaynell was struggling to walk, a sight that had motivated Frederick's chuckle.

Frederick smiled as he watched his wife, who was twenty-six years younger than him, take their daughter and rearrange her hair. While many an eyebrow had been raised when Frederick had married Percy, he didn't care. Percy made him happy, and vice versa. They were a good couple and had produced a beautiful daughter.

As the Wolfe family made their way through the train depot, Frederick spotted a newsstand. The ladies waited while he purchased a white rose and a piece of rock candy from the vendor. Walking back to his wife and daughter, Fredrick noticed he was sweating—a little ironic, he thought, considering it was such a cold day. He paused for a moment, produced a handkerchief from his pocket, wiped his brow, and then continued to Gaynell and Percy, who received his spontaneous gifts with beaming smiles. The final call for boarding sounded, and the time had come to say goodbye, for now anyway.

"I love you," Percy whispered in her husband's ear.

Gaynell scampered to her feet, ran to her mother and father, and squeezed them about the waist. She buried her head in the safety of her father's tummy. Both mother and daughter began to cry; then the sadness of the moment captured Frederick, and he began to cry as well.

The train whistle sounded. Frederick walked alongside the car, waving to his women. When he reached the end of the walkway, he stopped and smiled. *I love you*, he mouthed.

Percy smiled and nodded. Gaynell mouthed back through the train window, *I love you too, Daddy*.

Frederick stood at the edge of the concourse until the train disappeared from his sight. Making his way through the train station, Frederick began to bundle himself, in preparation for the elements awaiting him outside. Once again, however, Fredrick found himself sweating, this time more profusely than before. As he pulled the handkerchief from his pocket to wipe his forehead, a sharp, stabbing pain encompassed his chest. The pain caused Frederick to fall to the ground, where his body shook violently for a moment, then went limp. Fewer than two minutes after seeing his wife and child off for better days in California, Frederick Wolfe died of a massive heart attack.

A representative of the railroad met Percy Wolfe when the train arrived in Los Angeles and told her that her husband had passed away in Chicago. In an instant, Percy and Gaynell Wolfe's lives had changed. Percy and Gaynell were all alone.

It was a thought that horrified Percy Wolfe.

* * * * *

Spring 1912

Frederick's death created a void in Percy's life, and while she enjoyed her daughter's company, Percy was like most other adults. She needed adult companionship. Enter Virgil Gaylord.

Very little is known about Virgil Gaylord, probably since Gaylord is a man best forgotten. What is known is that Gaylord was a drunk—and a mean one at that. As a consequence of his drinking, Gaylord never held steady employment. When he did have a job, it usually didn't take too long for him to upset his employer by not showing up for work, fighting with other employees, or stealing from those who had hired him.

With Gaylord being such a jerk, it seems confusing that Percy Wolfe, lonely or not, would have any association with such a man. However, by August of 1912, Virgil Gaylord and Percy Wolfe had married.

Gaynell was twelve years old at the time of her mother's marriage to Gaylord. That relationship was the impetus for a great deal of the heartache and pain that Gaynell suffered as a teen.

As mentioned, Gaylord was a mean drunk. It wasn't too long after he had married Percy that he established himself as a wife-beater, as well. It became commonplace for Percy to suffer both verbal and physical abuse. Percy tolerated her husband's explosive behavior. She felt she had to, simply because she had no other options in life.

Gaylord's anger eventually found its way to Gaynell.

"The first time my step-father beat me was on a Saturday morning," Gaynell once said. "I had been in a hurry to play outside that day, and I forgot to make my bed, one of my daily chores. I came back in for lunch, and when I did, my stepfather exploded in a fit of rage.

"It was horrible, but in looking back on things, if he had not beaten me that day, I wouldn't have run away. If I hadn't run away, I might never have met Flossy. It was a strange chain of events. Perhaps it was divine intervention that had me running smack-dab into the Rockwell family's life.

* * * * *

Florence "Flossy" Rockwell was an enterprising young lady. At fourteen years of age, she understood the concept of money, and also knew that, with eight brothers and sisters at home, if she wanted anything extra in her life, she was going to have to earn it.

Flossy had had her eye on a summer dress, in the window of a local store, for some time. She had been saving her money and doing extra chores but was still a few dollars short of the price tag. So, with the dog days of summer upon the residents of Los Angeles, Flossy had decided to capitalize on the ninety-eight-degree heat by selling lemonade for three cents a glass. Thanks to the blistering rays of the sun, Flossy's business venture was booming. Copper coins in hand, the children of her neighborhood flooded her lemonade stand.

As the day began to wind down, Flossy felt as if someone was watching her. She was right. Gaynell was sheepishly peeking at the young entrepreneur from behind one of the houses. Initially, Flossy thought this girl was merely a reluctant customer, so she poured a glass of her product and held it up in the air.

"The first glass is free," she said.

Gaynell darted back behind the house.

"Come on," Flossy said a little louder. "It's really, really good. If you help me carry my things home, I'll give you two glasses."

Gaynell poked her head back around the corner of the house, and then timidly approached Flossy. As Gaynell neared, Flossy noticed that Gaynell had a fat lip and there was blood on her dress. Flossy extended the glass of lemonade toward the scared-looking little girl. Gaynell hesitated.

"Go ahead," Flossy said. "It won't hurt ya!"

Gaynell took Flossy's invitation, then without delay chugged down the beverage. Unfortunately, the acid of the lemons mixed into the cuts in Gaynell's mouth, and for the next several minutes, her mouth burned like Hell's fire.

"Gaynell cried like a coyote howling at the moon," Flossy recalled, years later.

"It won't hurt me?" Gaynell screeched. "The hell you say!"

"Once the burn went away," Flossy continued, "we both began to giggle. I introduced myself to Gay, and she to me. Our friendship started that day. It was a great memory, well, at least for me it was. That day marked the beginning of a friendship that lasted for more than sixty years."

Gaynell helped Flossy pack her wagon with the things from the lemonade stand. The two girls pulled the little cart back to the Rockwell home, a few blocks away.

Gaynell was immediately accepted into the Rockwell family. Lorenzo and Flossy cleaned Gaynell up a bit, tended to her wounds, and then fed her dinner.

"That night, my father walked Gaynell to her home, and had a conversation with Gaynell's step-father," Flossy said. "Later in life, I learned that he told Gaylord, if he ever beat his daughter again, he would wait until Gaylord fell asleep, then come into his house and stick a shovel in his head. Even though father was much older than Gaylord, his threat worked. Gaylord never beat Gaynell again."

* * * * *

Fall 1919

Lorenzo 'Renny' Rockwell II was a ruggedly handsome man, who possessed a tremendous sense of self-confidence, and from early indications, should have lived a full and happy life. Renny was a solid craftsman and had been working in the construction business since he was eight years old. By 1919, Renny had established himself as a good contractor and had very little problem finding consistent work.

With his professional life going in a good direction, Renny's focus shifted toward establishing his personal life and starting a family. It came as no surprise to any member of the Rockwell family that Renny set his eyes on his older sister's best friend… Gaynell Wolfe. Renny was head-over-heels in love with Gaynell and had been so for many years. For Renny, marrying Gaynell was something he had wanted to do for some time.

Gaynell, while always enjoying his company, was not as enthusiastic about marrying Renny Rockwell. Since the death of her real father, Gaynell's life had been one of deprivation. When her mother had married Gaylord, any chance for a normal childhood had ended. There were no earthly pleasures: no birthday gifts, no Christmas celebrations, and simply no enjoyments of any sort. Gaynell began to crave materialistic things.

Renny could make Gaynell laugh, and she knew he would care for her to the best of his ability. She also knew that Renny did not have the burning desire inside him to obtain wealth and social status that she did. He did not want to become filthy rich. It was a weakness, which in Gaynell's eyes, made him an unsuitable suitor—for marriage purposes, that is. In the spring of 1919, however, Gaynell's world came crashing down upon her, and her outlook on life changed, at least superficially.

* * * * *

May 1919

It was a gorgeous spring day. Renny was making his way to Gaynell's home when he stopped at an open field and gathered a handful of wildflowers. While Renny had grown accustomed to taking flowers to Gaynell's house, today's arrangement was for Percy, who had been hospitalized due to complications from her having the flu. Gaynell and Renny had made Sundays at the beach a ritual. With Percy in the hospital, however, Renny insisted they stop in and see her first.

Renny reached the junk-cluttered yard of Virgil Gaylord's home and knocked on the door. He heard a noise stir from inside, then quiet. He knocked again.

Nothing! He knew Gaynell was expecting him. Where was she?

Renny cupped his hands and pressed his face against the glass window on the door. As he gazed into the house, Gaylord flung open the front door.

"What the fuck do you want?" he yelled.

Renny stepped back. "I'm looking for Gay," Renny stammered. "Is she here?"

Gaylord was drunk and was holding a freshly-opened bottle of whiskey in his hand. His clothes looked as if they had been worn for weeks. They were as dirty as the smell was poignant.

"Is Gay here, sir?" Renny asked again.

"The little bitch ain't goin' anywhere with you," Gaylord said. "So get that out of your mind, right now. Understand?"

Renny merely stared at Gaylord. Renny Rockwell knew if he wanted to he could kick Gaylord's ass, and on many occasions had given thought to do just that. That moment, the same thoughts crossed his mind.

Gaylord stared at the younger man for a moment, then slammed the door shut. Even though Renny had been through this routine numerous times before, he was still dumbfounded by Gaylord's behavior.

A moment later, Gaynell came from around the corner of the house. "I thought you'd never get here," Gaynell's voice called out. "Are you ready to go?"

Gaylord's voice boomed from inside the house. "Where the hell are you, goddamn it?"

"He never gets it," Gaynell said. "All I have to do is run from my bedroom, down the hall, into the living room, through the kitchen, out the door, into the backyard, and then escape through the back gate. It takes me about six seconds to go from my bed to the yard."

As Gaynell and Renny walked away from the house, Gaylord's ramblings could still be heard.

"He'll look for me for a while, and then pass out," she said.

Renny stopped walking and looked at Gaynell. Her beauty was in direct contrast to the unsightly reality of her surroundings. How could this be?

After a brisk, twenty-minute walk, Gaynell and Renny reached the hospital and headed for Percy's room on the second floor. The nurse on duty recognized the two teens and handed them each a cloth mask.

"Twenty minutes," she said. "She's doing better, but we don't want to tire her out."

When Gaynell and Renny entered the room, Percy greeted her two visitors with open arms. Gaynell kissed and hugged her mother, while Renny handed Percy the flowers he had picked that day.

"You are a true gentleman, Renny Rockwell," Percy said.

For the next thirty minutes, Renny and Gaynell sat by Percy's side, sharing gossip, laughs, and a few tender moments. When the nurse came in with the evening meal, she advised the two teens that their "twenty" minutes were up and that it was time for them to go. Gaynell and Renny said their goodbyes, left the room and headed off to the beach.

Percy looked at her dinner and grunted. She didn't feel very well, so instead of eating, she pushed her tray aside, snuggled up in her blanket, and fell asleep.

* * * * *

After spending a night of lovemaking on the beach, Renny returned Gaynell to her home. When reaching the front door, Renny engulfed Gaynell in a clutching embrace and then pulled away to gaze at the love of his life.

"Why not marry me, Gay?" Renny asked, for the fourth time that day.

Gaynell had hoped that her letting Renny make love to her on the beach that day might have put the matter to rest… for a while, at least. "Good night," Gaynell said with a smile, kissing him on the cheek. "Maybe tomorrow we can talk about it."

"Are you serious?" Renny asked.

Gaynell nodded her head yes. Renny returned her kiss on the cheek, then ran down the walkway, jumping with joy all the way down, until he disappeared into the darkness.

* * * * *

Gaynell was asleep when a freak thunderstorm rolled into Southern California. A sudden crack of lightning and blast of thunder interrupted the tranquility of the night and awakened her from her slumber.

As she sat up in her bed, she felt that something was amiss. A lightning flash exposed a figure standing in the doorway of her bedroom. Gaynell jumped in fright. She locked her gaze on the figure in the doorway. It was Virgil.

"God damn it," Gaynell snapped. "You scared the shit out of me."

Virgil, holding a half-empty bottle of whiskey in his hand, walked to Gaynell's bedside, looked down at her, took another sip of whiskey, and exposed his blackened teeth in an evil grin.

Gaynell knew what Virgil wanted. She tried to bolt from the bed, but her stepfather grabbed onto her hair and pinned her to the mattress. The glass bottle fell from his hand, hit the wooden floor, and shattered. The sound caused him to shift his attention away from the terrified girl, who suddenly sank her teeth into Virgil's hand. He screamed and released his grip.

Gaynell leaped off the bed, but Virgil again grabbed her, and slammed her against the wall, causing her to slide to the floor. He stood over the girl and began to unbuckle his belt. As he lowered his pants, Gaynell delivered a solid kick to his knee, causing him to crash to the floor in a heap.

She sprang to her feet and ran through the house. As she hit the tile floor in the kitchen, she slipped, sliding against the cabinets on the other side of the room. Gaynell tried to get up but was consumed by enormous pain. She looked at her feet. They were bloodied; a result of her stepping on the broken glass from Virgil's whiskey bottle.

She pulled a piece of glass from her foot, just as the kitchen door slammed open. Virgil entered and locked a crazed gaze upon Gaynell. She scrambled to get to her feet, but he moved quickly and grabbed her.

Panicked, Gaynell reached out for something to defend herself with. Her hand found the handle of an iron skillet, sticking out from the sink. Grabbing it firmly with both hands, she swung the metal pan as hard as she could. The skillet hit Virgil's head with a loud *clank*. With Virgil lying on the floor, Gaynell ran to the back kitchen door and stumbled from the house.

After running down the road a few hundred feet, she looked back at the house and realized that this place would never again be her home. She turned and ran to the only place that would be safe for her. She went to the Rockwell home.

* * * * *

The next morning, Gaynell and Renny went to the hospital. Upon their arrival, they discovered that an hour after their visit with Percy, she had passed away from a cardiac arrest, induced by complications associated with the flu. A hospital employee had notified Virgil Gaylord earlier in the evening, a fact that Virgil had failed to tell Gaynell.

Virgil was never heard from again. Rumor had it he had killed himself a few months after Percy's death. Gaynell could only hope the rumors were true.

It was a horrible time in Gaynell's life. She had no family left in the world to call her own—no family, that is, except the Rockwells. The Rockwell home had been Gaynell's home-away-from-home since the first day she'd met Flossy at the lemonade stand, and from this moment on, it was her home, period.

For years, any time a crisis had arisen in Gaynell's life, she'd run to Flossy. This time was no different.

"Gaynell wanted to know what to do about Renny," Florence Rockwell Clark once recalled. "It wasn't my place to tell her. I loved my brother and spoke highly of Renny during our conversation, but ultimately told Gay that her decision to marry or not marry had to come from her and had to be a matter of heart and mind."

Renny was sitting on the porch steps of his father's home, whittling on a piece of wood, when the back door opened, and Gaynell emerged and sat by his side.

"Ya still wanna marry me?" she asked.

Without responding, Renny engulfed Gaynell in a bear-like hug. She held Renny tightly, for a moment, then pulled away and initiated a very passionate, yet fearful, kiss.

Gaynell was afraid. She was afraid that marrying Renny might mean she had to give up her dreams of money, wealth, and social status… but she was more afraid to be alone.

Chapter Five
Early Los Angeles

In the 1920s, Southern California was one of the fastest growing regions in America. Hundreds of people a day were immigrating to the Los Angeles area. From 1920 to 1930, the city's population doubled, climbing from one million to 2.2 million citizens. Much of Los Angeles's growth can be attributed to a group of power brokers who were known as "The Breakfast Club."

The Breakfast Club consisted of movie moguls, bankers, real estate barons, members of the oil industry, educators, and a socially-elite, upper-class citizenry who wanted to see Los Angeles rival Chicago, New York, and San Francisco as a great American city. The Breakfast Club understood that the good citizens of Los Angeles liked to think they were a more genteel group of people than their Midwestern or East Coast counterparts.

Publicly, the men who made up the Breakfast Club cried out for their police department to void the city of her vices. Privately, however, those who were profiting from Southern California's amazing growth knew that acceptance of vice was a necessary evil if Los Angeles, and therefore their bank accounts, were going to prosper. The bottom line was that Angelinos were willing to overlook the private indulgences of their neighbors, provided those involved in any illegal or immoral activities practiced discretion.

As a consequence of this philosophy, city councilmen, district attorneys, members of the mayor's office, and the rank and file of the police department routinely accepted financial contributions, kickbacks, and bribes from prostitutes, bootleggers, and upstart members of organized crime. The first identifiable crime syndicate came about when a young, aggressive, University of Southern California graduate attorney, named Kent Kane Parrot, decided to take advantage of L.A.'s tolerance for vice.

In 1921, Parrot, a football star for the USC Trojans, became active in promoting George Cryer for mayor. When Cryer defeated Meredith Snyder in the elections of 1921, Kent Kane Parrot became one of the most powerful men in Los Angeles. Within weeks of Cryer's election, Parrot pulled together a group of men who became the founding fathers of organized crime in the City of Angels. While none of the men in Parrot's gang had any official ties to the Cryer administration, these men were calling many of the shots with regards to the illegal activities happening in Los Angeles at the time.

The frontman in the Cryer/Parrot mob was Charlie Crawford, the owner of the Maple Bar in downtown Los Angeles. Crawford had an understanding of how to create an alignment between the criminals, politicians, and the police. Prior to coming to Los Angeles, Crawford had run the same type of scam with the citizenry and politicians of Seattle.

Crawford's role in the Parrot gang was to run the day-to-day operations of the business. Prostitution, smuggling liquor, bookmaking, betting, and casino development also fell under Charlie's control.

Albert Marco was the muscle of Parrot's gang. A thug who had been with Crawford in Seattle, Marco was the perfect henchman. He collected bets, worked the streets, and acted as Parrot's man-about-town.

Guy McAfee was another Parrot associate. A one-time member of the LAPD's vice squad, McAfee's contacts with the police proved a very valuable resource.

George Cryer and Kent Kane Parrot took full advantage of an environment ripe for corruption. Within a few months, the illegal gambling and vice operations of Cryer and Parrot were making the men more money than they had ever imagined.

Cryer's first term in office was marked by wide head of vice, to take command of the Los Angeles Police Department. spread corruption, with the most unscrupulous organization being the Los Angeles Police Department. Even the chief of police was bribable and not immune to the temptations of sin; a case in point was Louis Oakes, who was L.A.'s top cop during Cryer's first term.

After Oakes's office had solved two very high-profile cases, one being the kidnapping of a Southern California socialite and the other the murder of a police officer, the chief became a celebrity of sorts. However, after he was photographed in his car with a half-empty bottle of whiskey in his hand and a woman on his lap, not even his extreme popularity could protect him from the wrath of moral extremists. Soon after the scandal was exposed, Oakes was forced to resign. He had violated the prime directive of vice in Los Angeles; he'd failed to show discretion.

Initially, the relationship between the mayor's office and the Breakfast Club worked well. However, as Cryer's first term in office began to wind down, the mayor's gang became greedy. Parrot wanted complete control of Los Angeles vice and decided to test the power of the men in suits.

Parrot convinced Cryer that their group had the political power to break the symbiotic relationship between the Breakfast Club and the mayor's office. Sadly for the mayor and his cronies, Parrot was wrong.

Prior to the elections of 1925, George Cryer sought and then received, the endorsement of the *Daily News* in his bid for re-election. Since the *Daily News* was the primary competitor of the *Los Angeles Times*, Harry Chandler, owner and publisher of the *Times* and one of the most powerful members of the Breakfast Club, was outraged. Cryer's move caused Chandler to suspect that the mayor's group was attempting to break free from the influence of the Breakfast Club, which had been the real seat of power in Los Angeles since the turn of the century.

George Cryer wanted to branch out into areas previously controlled by the members of the Breakfast Club—real estate, water rights, and urban development were all areas controlled by the likes of Chandler, Hearst, and the other power brokers of the time. George Cryer wanted a more significant piece of the pie. The power play was on.

On election day, George Cryer was indeed chosen by the citizens of Los Angeles to serve another term as mayor. However, before too long, Cryer and his associates learned what a mistake they had made by trying to flex their political muscle. In the days following the election, the *Daily News* returned to business as usual. *The Los Angeles Times*, however, embarked upon a relentless journalistic attack on the mayor's policies and practices.

Harry Chandler had a tremendous influence on the lives of the citizenry of Southern California. Simply by deciding what was, or in some instances what was not, written about, Chandler imprinted his opinions onto the public in a way no one else could. While the *Times'* allegations of widespread corruption within city government was taken with a grain of salt by many Angelinos, George Cryer and Kent Kane Parrot quickly came to realize that Harry Chandler and the members of the Breakfast Club were never going to relent. These men were going to be an adversary that Cryer's administration could not defeat. Peace had to be made.

Cryer sought an audience with Chandler. The cost of peace with Chandler, for his administration, was the replacement of Chief of Police August Vollmer. The Breakfast Club wanted their favorite son, James Davis, who was the Commander of the Department's Vice Unit, to take command of the Los Angeles Police Department.

August Vollmer was committed to seeing that all people lived by the laws of the land, and his philosophy created problems for the men who were making their fortunes off bootlegging, gambling, and prostitution. Since Cryer and his men fell into this grouping, as well as Chandler's group, the demand for change was an easy concession for Cryer to make. By 1926, Vollmer was out as chief of police, and James Davis was in.

James Davis had joined the LAPD in 1912, made sergeant in 1921, lieutenant by 1922, and in 1924 was appointed as Commander of Vice. On the surface, Davis projected an image of high standards and impeccable character. His hard-core approach to police work pleased almost everyone, but as it turned out, Davis was as corruptible as any man.

For a short period of time, Angelinos were happy. The city was growing, the economy booming, and those who were a part of the corruption machine were making their fortunes.

City Councilman Carl Jacobson began to explore a variety of corruption allegations leveled against the L.A.P.D. During his investigation, Jacobson discovered that Albert Marco had indeed forced several women into a life of prostitution. Further, Jacobson determined that many of the higher-ups in the Los Angeles Police Department were profiting from Marco's operation.

The prostitution cartel attempted to buy the councilman's silence by offering him a $25,000 bribe. When Jacobson declined their offer, Marco and his friends in the L.A.P.D. decided to frame the councilman.

A constituent Jacobson knew as Helen Ferguson called the councilman one night, to talk about problems concerning a streetlight near her home. Jacobson agreed to come to the woman's residence and check into the situation. Shortly after Jacobson arrived at the woman's home, four police officers of Central Vice burst into the house, and the woman immediately claimed the councilman was in the process of assaulting her. Jacobson screamed his innocence.

As it turned out, the woman's name was not Helen Ferguson; rather, it was Callie Grimes, the sister-in-law of one of the arresting officers. The investigation of Mrs. Grimes revealed that Albert Marco had paid the woman a sum of money to lure Jacobson to her home and place him in a compromising position. The goal of the set-up was to frame the councilman on a trumped-up morals charge, which would, therefore, take the focus off the councilman's work against the prostitution ring.

The case against Jacobson was dismissed, and in the end, four members of Central Vice were forced to resign over the matter, including Harry Raymond, a veteran officer. Several years later, Raymond became a primary player in an even more amazing L.A. soap opera—the recall of future Los Angeles mayor, Franklin Shaw.

The false accusations against Jacobson and, more importantly, the fact that members of the LAPD were involved in the framing raised a few eyebrows. Still, the matter was not enough for Angelinos to scream for reform. Those voices would start to be heard after the arrest of a bootlegger named Harry McDonald.

After being arrested on vice charges, by a rookie police officer, McDonald decided to vent his frustration with the situation to a reporter from the *Daily News*. He stated to the press that he and Vice Commander Max Berenzweig had an arrangement that was supposed to keep his operation free and clear of police interference. After all, since McDonald was allegedly paying Berenzweig and several of his vice officers in excess of $100,000 a year, the criminal felt it was unfair he had been charged with a crime.

The *Daily News* jumped all over the story, and a series of articles on the corruption within the city government and the police force ensued. Despite all the allegations of wrong-doing against the Los Angeles Police Department, Angelinos remained calm and were still willing to be tolerant of vice taking place within their city.

The citizens' leniency, however, changed dramatically when Albert Marco shot a man on Venice Pier, and then attempted to bribe the arresting officer. To further complicate matters, Berenzweig skipped town, thereby confirming his guilt.

When many of the newspapers across the country began to portray Los Angeles as a den of iniquity, the citizens of Los Angeles decided they'd had enough. Cries for reform swept through the City of Angels like a Santa Ana wind. So, when a young deputy district attorney, named Dave Clark, and a grand jury foreman, named John Porter, convicted Albert Marco of multiple charges, then deported the muscle of the Cryer/Parrot gang back to Italy, Los Angeles had two new heroes.

The Cryer/Parrot gang had violated the first rule of vice in Los Angeles. They had forgotten that *discretion* was the hard, steadfast rule of vice and wrong-doing. As the elections of 1929 neared, George Cryer came under the gun.

* * * * *

Bob Shuler was a Virginia-born Methodist minister. As "Fighting Bob" saw it, Los Angeles was a sea of sin, in need of his personal salvation. By way of his Los Angeles-based radio station, KGEF, Shuler pitched a relentless, nightly attack on George Cryer.

Using every opportunity he could, Shuler accused the mayor and his administration of corruption at the most extreme levels. Shuler was backing John R. Porter, the jury foreman of the Marco trial, for mayor. After helping send Albert Marco away, Porter, a former auto-parts dealer, had become a champion for the people and was seen by Shuler as the man to lead Angelinos to a state of purity and righteousness that they all seemingly craved. Shuler's media blitz worked. Porter won the election and became mayor of Los Angeles.

With Marco's conviction and deportation, the McDonald fiasco, and Cryer's failed re-election, Charlie Crawford decided to skip town. Kent Kane Parrot tried to hold onto as much power as he could, but he knew that, sooner or later, there was going to be a changing of the guard with regards to Los Angeles vice. A blind man could see that Kent Kane Parrot's reign as king of vice in L.A. was coming to an end, but more importantly, so too could those elements of organized crime who were lining up at the table, ready to gobble down whatever scraps were left behind.

Bob Schuler was now the man behind the scenes, and the first favor the good Reverend asked of his newly-elected mayor was to serve him the head of James Davis on a platter. Schuler saw Davis as evil. The chief of police was removed from office.

If for no other reason than to show the citizens of Los Angeles that reform could be achieved swiftly, within a few days of his election, Porter reassigned Davis to the traffic department. Dick Steckel, the arresting officer in the Marco case, was appointed the new chief of police.

Fighting Bob's campaign against those he perceived to be immoral influences on society was brisk. Initially, the average citizen welcomed Shuler's attacks on corruption, vice, and lack of moral behavior. Most citizens probably would have tolerated Shuler's charge against sin, but when Fighting Bob turned his verbal blasting on two prominent, and very respected, members of the Breakfast Club, public opinion of Fighting Bob began to waver.

Rufus Von KleinSmid, president of the University of Southern California and Lois Pantages, of Pantages Theatre fame, came under Schuler's airway attacks. Schuler was unhappy with Von KleinSmid for allowing the theory of evolution to be taught at USCtherefore Porter, had to go. and disgusted with Lois Pantages for being charged with drunk driving, an allegation that later proved to be false.

The Breakfast Club took exception to Shuler's blast at their friends. Harry Chandler expressed his concerns over the matter to both Porter and Schuler, but despite Chandler's request for "vocal leniency," Schuler continued his radio attacks. The Breakfast Club decided Schuler, and therefore Porter had to go.

Chandler made some calls to a friend of his in the Federal Radio Commission, and soon after, Shuler became the target of a formal investigation for misuse of airwaves. Within a few months, Schuler was found guilty of the charges against him, sighted as an irresponsible broadcaster, and had his license revoked.

Without airtime, Shuler's popularity diminished, and Fighting Bob disappeared from the public eye. By crossing the Breakfast Club, Porter's chances for re-election in 1933 were minimal, and his administration began to crumble.

During Porter's stay in City Hall, Guy McAfee had tried to increase his stake in gambling and prostitution. However, McAfee's ability to keep control of his empire was being challenged daily by upstart-mobster Jack Dragna. Even Charlie Crawford reappeared in Los Angeles, for a short period of time.

Crawford sensed the changing of the political guard in Los Angeles and returned to Southern California in late 1930. Charlie's hope was to get back in cahoots with McAfee and seek to establish control of the rackets in Los Angeles with the election of 1933.

Even though McAfee was having trouble controlling his gambling interests, he was not warm to the idea of getting involved with Crawford again. So Guy refused Charlie's offer of re-establishing their relationship, which, in turn, caused Charlie to vow to bring McAfee down.

Crawford and his new partner, Herb Spencer, founded a magazine called the *Critic of Critics*, a publication that proved to be an excellent avenue for Crawford to attack McAfee with every edition. Fighting Bob Schuler had shown Crawford how powerful the media could be, and Charlie probably would have been successful in his bid to see McAfee fall, if he had not been murdered.

Charlie Crawford's killer came into the office of the *Critic of Critics* and shot both Crawford and Spencer dead. Initially, Guy McAfee was the prime suspect in the double homicide. However, much to the surprise of everyone, Dave Clark, the district attorney in the Marco trial, had killed Crawford and Spencer for what Clark labeled "self-defense" reasons.

Clark stated that Crawford wanted the former deputy district attorney to help him frame Los Angeles Chief of Police Dick Steckel. When Clark refused, the two men argued. Crawford pulled a gun; Clark pulled a gun. Shots were exchanged, and Crawford ended up dead. After killing Crawford, Clark noticed Spencer coming at him, and shot him, too—all in self-defense, mind you.

Dave Clark was arrested for the murder of the two men, tried, and found not guilty. In the years following the murders, Clark lived in a big, fashionable home and never had money problems. Some speculate Jack Dragna was responsible for Crawford's demise. This theory would have some validity, especially when you consider while McAfee was absolved of all wrong-doing in the Crawford/Spencer killings, his ability to work anonymously was effectively over.

The winds of change for control over racketeering in Southern California were blowing. The only question was who would take control of the City of Angels' most lucrative business venture—the business of sin.

Chapter Six

The Italians-Friends of Ours

J ack Dragna was born Ignatius Dragna in Corleone, Sicily, in 1891. At the age of seven, Dragna and his parents had immigrated to the United States. By 1908 however, the elder Dragnas had decided to return to their native land and had taken their children with them.

In 1914, Dragna, then twenty-three years old, had returned to the United States. Within a year of his return to California, he was convicted of extortion and sent to San Quentin prison where he served 6 months of a three year.

In 1918, Dragna went to work for Joseph Ardizzone; a man regarded as the first Italian of organized crime in Los Angeles. Ardizzone was an unassuming boss, with little desire to be a mover and shaker. As an underling to Ardizzone, Dragna was forced to accept a minimal role in the Los Angeles vice rackets. In the mid-'20s, however, Jack Dragna got into the game when he became the head of an immigration rights organization, called the Italian Welfare League (IWL).

The IWL was developed to protect the interests of the Italian working class. They held nightly language classes and helped Italians with naturalization process plus provided legal counsel and translators; it was also the avenue by which Jack Dragna would lay the foundation for his criminal empire.

* * * * *

Spring 1923

Los Angeles was a city growing by leaps and bounds. Construction in Los Angeles, in 1919, had totaled made reference to 28 million dollars. In 1920, the figure had climbed to $60 million, and in 1921, the city issued $121 million in construction contracts.

Southern California was booming, and Los Angeles was handing out hundreds of thousands of dollars in building contracts. As a consequence of this evolution, Mayor George Cryer and Jack

Dragna entered into a back-room arrangement, away from the eyes and pocketbooks of their respective associates, which allowed both men to make a small fortune.

Dragna and Cryer developed a method to exploit the issuance of city construction contracts. Since the IPL controlled many of the workers during the early and mid-'20s, they also controlled labor costs. Construction companies, endorsed by the IPL, made lower bids than their competitors. As a consequence, many of the city contracts went to IPL-sanctioned companies. After securing the winning bid for city contracts, contractors kicked back a percentage of the projects' profits to Dragna, who, in turn, made donations back to the mayor's office, via the Italian Protective League. Through his arrangement with Cryer, Dragna built a financial base that enabled him to grease the palms of city council members, assistant district attorneys, and street cops.

When George Cryer was voted out of office and replaced with John Porter, Dragna's influence over organized crime increased. The crackdown that Porter brought on corruption within the Los Angeles Police Department had a domino effect on the rank-and-file officer. As upper management was fired, those in the ranks were elevated in position.

Dragna had been networking with the street cops of the LAPD since the early 1920s, so by the early 1930s, Dragna had several street cops on his payroll. As Mayor Porter began removing many of the higher-ranking members of the police department, the Dragna-influenced beat cops were elevated in rank, into positions of greater power.

Jack Dragna's biggest break came after the elections of 1933 when Franklin Shaw was crowned the new mayor of Los Angeles. Shaw and Dragna had been longtime friends, and with Shaw in office, Dragna was assured a larger piece of the vice pie.

* * * * *

It seems ironic that the mention of Jack Dragna's reign as the godfather of early Los Angeles crime often earns chuckles. Most people seem to think Dragna's career as a crime boss was an under-achievement. Nothing could be further from the truth.

While Dragna never attempted to exploit Los Angeles the way the bosses of New York or Chicago did, Dragna sensed that organized crime in the West couldn't be run the same way that it was back on the East Coast or in the Midwest. Dragna, with his seemingly non-assuming attitude, was a perfect fit for Southern California, where residents wanted to appear sophisticated, yet, still have their vices satisfied; discretely, that is.

Dragna's organization was criticized for making only modest profits. However, during the heyday of Dragna's influence over Southern California vice (the early '30s through the mid-'40s), he controlled over three hundred gambling halls, over twenty thousand slot machines, almost two thousand bookies, and at least five hundred brothels—all of which made a tidy profit. Organized crime's take from vice, during the '30s and '40s, was said to be at nearly fifty million dollars a year.

Dragna was also criticized for the way rival mobsters, especially those with East Coast ties, were allowed to enter Los Angeles undisputed and unchallenged. While this may have been true, mobsters with the more prolific personalities, such as Mickey Cohen or Benjamin Siegel, never established their roots in the City of Angels, and either ended up in jail (Cohen) or murdered (Siegel).

Jack Dragna spent very little time behind bars and he died of natural causes on February 23, 1956.

While Los Angeles Police Chief Daryl Gates is credited for coining the phrase – The Mickey Mouse Mafia (in regard to the LA mobsters) some time after Dragna's death, in the early 1970s, this author's eventual great-uncle, Nick Moretta, made reference to Dragna's organization being labeled with the same nickname – "Mickey Mouse Mafia." Nick chuckled, then stated "the reference must be some type of complement; after all, does anybody realize how much money that fuckin' mouse makes in a year?" His point should be well taken.

*****

Nicholas V. Moretta was born on September 15, 1901, in Bari, Italy. Shortly after his birth, the Moretta family immigrated to the United States and settled in the Los Angeles area. It didn't take

Mrs. Moretta long to strike up several friendships, and one of the people she made friends with was the mother of one Jack Dragna.

"My parents had family from Corleone," Nick once said. "When Mom and Mrs. Dragna discovered they had a common bond, their friendship took off."

After Jack Dragna was released from San Quentin prison, in 1915, he returned to Los Angeles. Due to their continuing relationship with Dragna's parents, when Jack arrived back in the old neighborhood, the Morettas looked in on Jack from time to time. Thus, a friendship was formed between the Moretta family and Jack Dragna.

In 1919, Nick Moretta was a typical eighteen-year-old. Impressed by Dragna, Nick aspired to be a gangster and began working for Dragna on low-profile profit-making opportunities, such as number running, marking patsies for games of chance, and doing general errands.

While Nick made some money, it wasn't enough to make a living, so by the early '20s, he'd begun working odd jobs in the construction industry, as well. It was during that time that Nick landed a position with Rockwell Construction. Lorenzo Rockwell took an instant liking to Moretta, as did Rockwell's sons, Renny, Homer, and Guy. Since the entire Rockwell family was involved in the construction business, they were always in need of general labor help, which provided Nick with steady work. In the early 1920s, the relationship Nick Moretta had with Rockwell Construction, and Jack Dragna caused the two groups to come together in a business arrangement, which proved to be beneficial to all three parties.

"Renny Rockwell was a construction contractor," Nick once said. "Jack had a very nice arrangement involving the issuance of construction contracts with the city, so getting Renny and Jack together seemed to me like an opportunity for all of us to make some money."

"Renny had an excellent reputation as a general contractor. The contracts Renny landed were all above-board and legitimate. Renny's bids were always honest, so the fact that he won a significant number of the contracts came about for several reasons, not just because of his connection with Jack.

"If Renny had been a poor contractor, he never would have had a chance at getting the jobs. On the other hand, if Renny had not known Jack, he wouldn't have had a chance, either. It just seemed that, after I introduced Jack and Renny, everything seemed to work out.

"At first, getting Renny to meet Jack was a pain in the ass. I had been trying to arrange a meeting between them for several weeks, but Renny was reluctant to talk with him, because of Jack's reputation of being a mobster."

The truth of the matter was that Rockwell Construction was securing a number of jobs, which in turn were allowing the family to make a modest income. While Renny was happy with the finances of the family, Gaynell, now his wife, wanted more. In her eyes, without obtaining a few big-time construction contracts, she would never have the material things she wanted, and would, therefore, be forced to live an inconsequential existence.

"I knew going into business with Dragna would be profitable," Gaynell once said. "But I also knew there was a possibility the arrangement would be illegal. I thought the trade-off was worth it. Renny, however, had reservations, which were probably manifested in his hesitation to meet Jack. While we debated whether or not Renny was even going to talk to Dragna, let alone do business with him, in the end, I was able to convince him to meet with Dragna and listen to his proposition."

At Gaynell's request, Nick arranged for Renny to meet with Jack Dragna in a downtown Los Angeles restaurant. During the meeting, Jack explained how things were going to work and how simple a process it was.

"Jack told Renny that an agent of his would provide him with a monthly list of city construction contracts to bid on," Gaynell said. "If any of the jobs appealed to Renny, and he bid on them and won the bid, all that Renny was obliged to do was to pay Jack a finder's fee.

"Since the jobs on Jack's list would triple Renny's profits and his business, it seemed like a win-win situation for Rockwell Construction. Renny accepted Jack's proposal. That was how we became involved with Jack Dragna."

While Renny initially had reservations about working through Jack Dragna, as job after job rolled in, he became more and more at ease with doing business through Dragna. Jack Dragna never tried to put the squeeze on Rockwell or change the conditions of the deal. In fact, during Rockwell Construction's tenure with Dragna, the company secured work on a number of city projects, including the construction of many of downtown Los Angeles' sidewalks, several city-sponsored residential housing tracts, and the Atlantic Richfield building.

Rockwell Construction was flourishing. With their newly-found success, Gaynell was confident that it was only a matter of time before the life of affluence she craved would be forever hers.

Chapter Seven
Through Adversity...Comes a Friendship

Harry Clark was born on February 13, 1898, in Pawtucket, Rhode Island. He came to California in 1923. Harry, a World War I veteran, was a cement-and-concrete man who moved west to take advantage of Los Angeles' booming construction industry.

Within days of his arrival in Southern California, Harry had found work with Rockwell Construction, and it wasn't too long before Harry found love with Florence "Flossy" Rockwell, the boss's sister. On August 3, 1923, the couple married, and on July 17, 1925, Flossy gave birth to their first child, Marion.

"When Marion was born, Betty Ann was only two years old," Flossy said. "It was evident from day one that the two girls had something special between them. The first time Betty Ann saw Marion, she lit up like a Christmas tree.

"Early in Marion's life, there were times where I had all three of the kids, my one and Gaynell's two," Flossy said.

"Bob was the oldest, a sweet boy with a pleasant disposition. I could tell at an early age that he was going to be a real charmer and a smart businessman. He was polite and street-smart, and if I ever needed help with the two girls, I could count on Bob, even at a young age, to help out.

"Betty Ann was a handful. She had a personality on her, and when it combined with that inquisitive mind of hers, she could be a pistol. Marion was the baby of the group. She was going to be influenced by her cousins, so I was pleased that Bob and Betty Ann had great qualities.

"Renny and Gaynell were always busy, so it just seemed natural to pitch in and watch the children from time to time. Renny was my brother, Gaynell was my friend, and I would have done anything for either one of them.

"While I always thought Gaynell and I were close, we were brought even closer when Renny became sick. I was Renny's closest sibling, and Gaynell was his wife. We were both completely devastated when he turned up sick, and even more so when he passed away."

* * * * *

For years, everyone had thought Renny's persistent cough was a natural by-product created by the inhalation of dust and debris from working in the construction trade. No one attributed it to something more serious, and no one would have imagined that, at the age of twenty-seven, Renny would have tuberculosis.

"In the late '20s, Renny Rockwell entered the Pottinger Sanitarium," Gaynell once said. "Pottinger was located in Southern California and was known for its treatment of tuberculosis patients. At the time, we had no idea what to do, so we just sought the best treatment money could buy."

While the sanitarium offered comfort for Renny, doctors offered very little hope. Treating Renny's illness was expensive, and the once-impressive Rockwell savings quickly disappeared, forcing Gaynell to seek work for the first time in her life.

She found work as a secretary for the City of Los Angeles, where she was a member of the general secretarial pool. While times were difficult, she worked hard to make sure the needs of her children were met. That meant time away from home, which also meant that the Rockwell children, Bob, and Betty Ann, had to be cared for.

Gaynell went to Flossy for help, something she would do for the remainder of her life. By that time, Flossy had given birth to her second child, Gene. The responsibility of watching over all four children became Florence's lot in life. It was something she enjoyed and did not once complain about having to do.

Like Renny, Harry Clark was a construction man. Unlike Renny, however, Harry was not under the Dragna sphere of influence. Translation: Harry was not landing large construction contracts and, like most construction contractors in Los Angeles, he was barely making ends meet.

Despite the Clarks' financial shortcomings, when Gaynell needed Flossy, she was there for her sister-in-law. Flossy took the Rockwell children into her home and cared for them as if they were her own. During Renny's illness, the Rockwell and Clark children were together night and day, allowing Marion and Betty Ann to build a foundation for their lifelong friendship.

"By 1929, Mom and Gaynell were spending as much time as possible with Renny," Marion said. "He was at Pottinger, and as a consequence, Betty Ann and I were together all the time. We ate together, slept together, and bathed together. Good God, how we bathed together!

"It wasn't any surprise Betty Ann and I developed a close relationship," Marion continued. "Mom and Gaynell were like sisters, so I think it was natural for Betty Ann and m to have a similar relationship.

"Betty Ann was like a big sister to me. She looked out for me and protected me. It was a role she took very seriously and was very good at doing."

An example of Betty Ann's protective instinct came during a frightening incident involving a "peeping tom." The peeper was the brother of Leonard Sly, also known as Roy Rogers, one of the most famous cowboy movie stars of our time.

The Slys were from Oklahoma. Like many Americans of the time, they were a dirt-poor family who had come to California to escape the harsh economy created by drought and the Great Depression.

"When the Sly family moved to town, it looked like a scene from *The Grapes of Wrath*," Marion said. "Their pick-up truck was loaded with crates, furniture, and even the kitchen sink. Life was tough for everyone during that time, but things were especially hard on the Slys.

"On the evening in question, Betty Ann was spending the night. We were both sound asleep when a sound from outside our bedroom window woke me up. When I looked up, I saw a pair of eyes staring at me. I couldn't move. I was terrified.

"While I didn't say a word or even move, Betty Ann awoke, looked at me, and asked what was wrong. When I didn't answer, she tracked my eyes to the window and saw the boy looking down on us. Betty Ann picked up a vase that was sitting on the nightstand and threw it toward the window. The crashing glass woke up everyone in the house. I yelled for help. Betty Ann sprang from bed, ran out of the room, and took off after the culprit.

"My dad and Betty Ann found the boy hiding under our car, which was parked in the driveway. After discovering the young man was one of the Sly boys, my father gave the boy a severe tongue-lashing, then sent him home.

"Betty Ann was just eight but was unyielding in her suspicion that the boy was up to something more than peeking in windows. My father chuckled at Betty Ann's suspicions, then tucked us into bed. The next day, when my father went outside to the chicken coop to gather eggs for breakfast, he discovered what the Sly boy had been up to—chicken thieving.

"The Sly boy, my father had captured, was acting as a distraction for another brother who had broken into our chicken coop and taken our birds. My father called the authorities, who recovered all but a few of the chickens.

"Later that evening, Leonard (Roy Rogers) came to our house with a freshly-baked apple pie in one hand and a kettle of chicken potpie in the other. It was Roy's way of apologizing."

Another scary event in the lives of the two girls came at their favorite place, Redondo Beach. Harry Clark had taken both Marion and Betty Ann to the pier that day for some fun in the sun. At the time, the Redondo Beach roller coaster was one of the biggest and fastest on the West Coast. The girls had worked up enough courage to ride the roller coaster and Harry, while not much of a coaster enthusiast, had reluctantly agreed to chaperone the girls on their ride.

A few seconds into the ride, Harry knew that something was very wrong. The coaster rattled, shook, and shimmied in a way far different from any of the previous experiences Harry had had on thrill rides. It took all he had to keep the girls in the car during the ride.

When the ride concluded, Harry complained to workers that the ride was rough and dangerous. Tragically, Harry's disapproval of the ride fell on deaf ears. Three trips later, the coaster broke away from the track and crashed into the ocean, killing a number of riders.

"In 1930," Marion recalled, "we began spending more and more time at Pottinger with Uncle Renny. We didn't understand then how precious our time with him was. We just knew we never looked forward to the aftermath of those visits.

"After each visit with Renny, we were bathed from head to toe with Lysol disinfectant. It was awful. The smell of fake pine was implanted in our noses forever. Needless to say, we hated the smell of Lysol, and neither Betty Ann nor I ever used the disinfectant in our homes.

"There was something about going through the tough times that brought Betty Ann and me together. Our experiences as kids, the good and the bad, made our friendship that much more special."

In the fall of 1930, Betty Ann and Marion would share their first real-life tragedy, when at the age of thirty, Renny Rockwell lost his battle with tuberculosis. It was the first time either girl had experienced death.

Renny's passing created a serious dilemma for Gaynell; she was a widow, a single mother who was still yearning to achieve wealth, power, and social status. With Renny, Gaynell was on her way to satisfying the materialistic things she craved. Without him, she was back to square one, but she didn't stay there for very long.

"Renny's death put into motion a bizarre series of events," Marion recalled. "In a lot of ways, I think if Renny hadn't have died, the things that happened in Gaynell's life from 1930 on would have never happened. Gaynell wouldn't have felt forced to do certain things. Who knows? Maybe our lives would have turned out differently than they did."

Chapter Eight
Franklin Shaw"Hiz Honor Da Mayor"

Franklin L. Shaw was born on February 1, 1877. Shaw's parents, John D. and Katherine Roche Shaw, were residents of War-wick, a province of Ontario, Canada.

In 1883, the Shaws immigrated to the United States and eventu-ally settled in Joplin, Missouri. In 1897, Shaw's father passed away and Franklin, at the age of twenty, became the family's primary source of income. For the next several years, he worked as a sales-man for the Campbell-Redell Wholesale Grocery Company. He enjoyed being a salesman and was very good at shaking hands and winning over new clients.

Shaw next became the general manager for the Ozark Coal and Railroad Company, based in Fort Smith, Arkansas. While Shaw's stay in Fort Smith was only a few years in length, it was significant in that he met his future bride there, Cora H. Shires, whom he married on February 5, 1905.

By 1909, Shaw was a representative of the by-products depart-ment of the Cudahy Packing Company. His business brought him to California. Shaw liked the mild winters offered by the California climate and became the company's West Coast representative.

Through the course of his life, Shaw was a member of several clubs and learned societies, including the Masons, Elks, Shriners, Knights of Pythias, United Commercial Travelers of America, Moose, Eagles, and the Maccabbe. He was also a member of the Los Angeles Athletic Club, the Church of Brotherhood of America, and a Los Angeles-based organization called the Breakfast Club.

In 1919, Shaw went to work for Haas-Baruch and Company of Los Angeles, California. Again, he put to use his personality to make friends and influence people. It was during his time as a sales-man that Shaw first captured the attention of Jack Dragna.

The Italian workers of a wholesale grocery store had a conflict with the management at one of the company's warehouses. Dragna, as the president of the Italian Protective League (I.P.L.), was called to the site to intervene. Once Dragna arrived, however, he discovered a wholesale salesman named Franklin Shaw had already facilitated an agreement between the workers and the management. Shaw needed the immediate delivery of an order and knew the only way to get what he wanted was to facilitate a peace between the two parties. His quick thinking and handling of the situation impressed Dragna. From that point on, Franklin Shaw and Jack Dragna were connected.

Dragna had seen Kent Kane Parrot work behind the scenes of George Cryer's administration to make him a fortune and knew if he was going to achieve real power in Los Angeles, he had to have contacts in City Hall. Dragna was on the hunt for up-and-coming politicians who he could bring into his fold. Shaw was a perfect fit for his master scheme.

In 1925, Shaw decided to run for political office. With the support of the Italian Protective League, who provided help with pep rallies and door-to-door solicitations of voters, he was elected to the Los Angeles City Council of the 8th District. During Shaw's first term on the City Council, he and Dragna entered into several under-the-table arrangements and formed a corrupt alliance that remained in place for almost fifteen years.

Shaw and Dragna's first arrangement together involved the sale of groceries to city-sponsored facilities. The scam was simple: A produce company with ties to Dragna would obtain city-sponsored contracts to supply fresh fruit and vegetables to various city facilities, primarily hospitals. The companies with ties to Dragna would pay top dollar for aged produce from Shaw's old employers. The produce company would, in turn, sell its product to the city hospitals at a highly-inflated price. Dragna and Shaw would then split the profit. The arrangement bilked the City of Los Angeles out of thousands of dollars a day.

* * * * *

Through the early and mid-'20s, Harry Chandler and the other members of the Breakfast Club had been able to manipulate the policies and practices of the city government to accommodate their interests. Toward the end of George Cryer's second term in office, it had become clear that his administration had felt strong enough to break free from the influence of the Breakfast Club, while at the same time ignoring the rule of vice in L.A.

As the elections of 1928 approached, the Breakfast Club had made one decision, and that was that Cryer had to go. The Club was not to be tested, nor betrayed. While they had no candidate of their own, the group began to support the reform candidate, John Porter.

The wrong-doing of Cryer's administration was suddenly brought to light in the public arena, causing the gentry of Los Angeles to clamor for change. Cryer's power-play had backfired, and his term as mayor came to an end on November 28, 1928, when John Porter was elected.

John Porter ran on a platform of clearing Los Angeles of her social ills and sicknesses, gambling, and vice. Initially, the concept of cleaning up their city appealed to many Angelinos.

The election of 1928 marked the changing of the guard in Southern California's organized crime structure. Even though Kent Kane Parrot still held control of many of the vices in Los Angeles, his seat of power was gone, and his grip on Los Angeles had begun to loosen. It was a situation that created a window of opportunity for one Jack Dragna.

While Dragna could have created a turf war with Cryer's gang, he instead chose to run a quiet operation. Along with a handful of fellow mobsters, he opened up a number of gambling ships off the Southern California coast. Dragna's offshore operations, which included gambling, liquor, and prostitution, conducted carefully and away from the public eye, generated a hefty profit for him and his associates.

During John Porter's term as mayor, Dragna and Franklin Shaw engaged in a number of backroom deals that generated a nice income for both men. Shaw had won his bid to become the county supervisor for the 2nd District, and Dragna had gained full control of the Italian mob in Southern California, after the disappearance of his boss, Joe Ardizzone.

Ardizzone had mysteriously vanished in October of 1931, while on his way to visit relatives in Etiwanda, California. His disappearance was always suspected to have been by the hand of Dragna, though Jack always denied it. In any event, at a time when the rest of the country was suffering amidst an economic depression of enormous magnitude, Dragna and Shaw were making a small fortune off their behind-the-scenes deals.

When Porter began making good on his campaign promises to clean up Los Angeles, it didn't take long for the citizens of Los Angeles to realize vice, at least in moderation, wasn't all that bad and, in fact, may have been a good thing. After he refused to allow the chairman of the 1932 Olympic Games to give the traditional champagne toast to open the Los Angeles games, even conservative Angelinos began to think that John Porter's ideals were a bit too conservative to tolerate.

The Breakfast Club had lost some of its control during Porter's reign as mayor, so as the elections of 1933 approached, the members believed they had to find a candidate they could influence. They had their man when Franklin Shaw decided to run for mayor.

In 1933, Franklin Shaw seemed to be just what the people of Los Angeles needed. He was a politician who was willing to fight vice publicly, but also willing to understand the needs of the people. In June of 1933, he was elected mayor of Los Angeles.

Chandler had been lukewarm to Shaw during the mayoral campaign, but shortly after Shaw's election, he sought an audience with the newly-elected mayor. During their meeting, Chandler revealed to Shaw that he and his circle of friends had conducted private investigations on all the candidates of the 1933 mayoral campaign. Chandler's sleuths had discovered Shaw's entire political career had been laced with wrongdoing. From bribes to kickbacks, to campaign contributions from local mobsters, madams, and bootleggers, Chandler had enough dirt on Shaw's newly-born administration to topple it, if he'd desired to do so.

Much to Shaw's surprise, all Chandler wanted was for the new mayor to support specific Breakfast Club interests. If Shaw showed he was willing to work with the good ol' boys, they would support his political agendas and keep his indiscretions of the past confidential. The club's first request was for Shaw to reinstate James Davis, a Breakfast Club favorite, as chief of the Los Angeles Police Department.

Franklin Shaw must have thought he had died and gone to heaven. Shaw, Davis, and Jack Dragna had been in a secret alliance since the mid-'20s. When Shaw was a councilman and supervisor for the 2nd District, Davis was the commander of Vice and Dragna was already an underboss. Chandler's offer was a defining moment in Shaw's life.

Free from having the watchful eyes of Los Angeles' major newspaper locked on his every move, Shaw's administration was essentially given the green light to exploit Los Angeles in a way that no one else ever had before them. From 1933 to 1938, Shaw and his associates engaged in one money-making scheme after another.

In addition to the typical vices of prostitution, gambling, and liquor, Shaw's group influenced the hiring of city employees and controlled the promotions of members of the Los Angeles Police Department and the goings-on in the Coroner's Department. They also continued to engage in the manipulation of various city contracts, including construction contracts, school and hospital meal programs, and real estate speculations. Purchasing near-worthless properties, then re-zoning them into business districts, Shaw and his associates made windfall profits.

When Shaw took control of the mayor's office, Los Angeles was drowning in a pool of economic despair. The Depression had created an environment where the bread lines were long and makeshift, tar-papered huts were commonplace. Sadly, during Franklin Shaw's tenure in office, he did little to make things better for those who elected him. What Franklin Shaw did do, however, was take advantage of his position and establish his regime as one of the most corrupt administrations in Los Angeles political history.

Chapter Nine
A Deal with the Devil?

One of Marion Clark-Hull's earliest childhood recollections involved a monumental decision made by her Aunt Gaynell. "In the fall of 1933, Gaynell was at a crossroads in her life," Marion recalled. "Bob was twelve years old, Betty Ann was ten, and I was eight.

"After Uncle Renny had passed away, Gaynell had to work odd jobs. Most nights she didn't get off work until late, so Bob and Betty Ann had become fixtures at our house.

"I think one of the reasons my mother and Gaynell had such a strong bond was become Mom was so willing to care for Gaynell's children while she worked. Mom had grown accustomed to watching the kids since the late '20s when Renny had first got sick. Initially, I think, Gaynell felt guilty about having Mom raise her children, but as time passed, she came to accept things and realized if she was going to survive, having Mom watch Bob, and Betty Ann was the way things had to be.

"As kids, we loved being together. On summer nights, we would play outside until it became dark, and then come in for a late-night snack—usually a piece of hot, sweet bread with honey.

"When it was time for bed, Bob, Betty Ann, my brother Gene, and I would all lie upon my parents' bed and chatted for hours. We would giggle, talk, and then giggle some more, until we all fell asleep. Mom said we looked like a litter of puppies all snuggled up against each other.

"Most nights, Gaynell would get to the house late, peek into the bedroom, and then return to the kitchen, where Mom would heat up whatever was left over from dinner. Gaynell would sit at the kitchen table and eat, while Mom would pour herself a cup of tea, grab a chair, and then sit and listen to Gaynell talk about her day's experiences.

"Gaynell was a great gossip, and Mom made the perfect audience. Mom was what is today called an effective listener. A woman who seldom said much, Mom's lot in life was to be there for her sister-in-law.

"On some nights, Betty Ann and I would sneak out of our beds, press our ears near the crack in the door, and eavesdrop on our mothers' conversations. Our mothers were such gossips and, while much of the time we had no understanding of the context of what they were talking about, we still enjoyed being the snoops that we were.

"I learned at an early age what a turning point was—those times in our lives when the decisions we make will lead us down one future path or another. Some people can point to a specific time in their lives and say that an event or a decision had significant ramifications on the rest of their lives. Gaynell was one of those people. She had a turning point in her life, and it came one evening in 1933, shortly after the election of Franklin Shaw as the mayor of Los Angeles."

* * * * *

"I don't like this," Gaynell said, sitting at the Clark dinner table. "I work my ass off, and for what?"

Flossy shrugged her shoulders.

"God damn it, Flossy, I'm tired of being poor. I'm sick of it. I work all day, most of the night. I never get to see my kids, and for what? A few dollars a month!"

"I know times are tough," Flossy responded. "But hell, you basically ran Rockwell Construction. You have typing skills, you know how to keep books, you know…"

"I can get a job with the new mayor," Gaynell interrupted.

Flossy's eyebrows shot into the air. "With Shaw?" she asked.

Gaynell nodded her head yes. "I would have to do a lot of different things," she said. "But I'd be willing to do whatever they asked."

"Hell, Gay," Flossy said, "you're smart. You can pick up on most anything. You don't need to do nothing you don't want to."

Gaynell seemed reserved. "Jack Dragna would be the one who could make this happen," she said.

"Oh," Flossy said a slight hint of alarm in her voice.

An uncomfortable silence consumed the room. Flossy got up, walked to the stove, and grabbed the coffee pot. She came back to the table and refilled the cups.

"Ya sure ya wanna do something like that, Gay?" she asked.

Tears started to roll down Gaynell's cheeks. "If I don't, I'll never get the things I want," she said.

Gaynell began to cry. Flossy embraced Gaynell from behind and held her tightly.

"I'm done being poor, Flossy," Gaynell said. "I'm done with it, period. I don't give a shit what I have to do to get nice things. I'd sell my soul the devil if I had to, to get what I want."

Flossy held her sister-in-law tighter. She knew Gaynell had made up her mind. She was going to work for Shaw.

Years later, Gaynell identified her decision to go to work for Shaw as the "date of conception for the horrible tragedy that came to be on September 13, 1947. Had I not gone to work at the mayor's office, maybe I wouldn't have become involved in the things I did," Gaynell said. "Maybe I wouldn't have met the people that I met, and maybe Betty Ann would still be with us."

* * * * *

"I'm not really sure when Gaynell started to work for Franklin Shaw or what her official capacity was," Marion recalled. "I do know that by the 1930s the perks of her job had an impact on all of us.

"Gaynell had gone from rags to riches almost overnight. It wasn't any time before she had purchased a home in the Valley, a new car, and had an entirely new wardrobe to wear. Despite their new home, Betty Ann and Bob still ended up staying with us a great deal of the time, so the important things hadn't changed all that much. We were still a family.

"Gaynell never shared the details of her job with us, but even at eleven years old, I knew something was amiss. Gaynell's willingness to sacrifice her scruples created an inner turmoil for her that caused a dark cloud to hang over her head. While she seemed happy with the material things, she never seemed happy with herself."

* * * * *

While Gaynell may have seemed to have some moral reservations about her association with Shaw's group, she nonetheless reaped the benefits of being a member of the most corrupt political machine in the history of Los Angeles.

During the mid-'30s, the population of Los Angeles was booming. And so, too, were the number of deaths. In addition to bilking the living by working the vices of booze, prostitution, and gambling, Shaw's administration was also raiding the estates of those who'd passed away. It was in this arena that Gaynell served Shaw's group almost daily.

Whenever a death occurred in Los Angeles, the police would respond. They would then contact the coroner's office, which in turn would contact someone in the mayor's office. More often than not, the person in City Hall who was contacted was Gaynell Rockwell. Gaynell and whichever coroner was on duty would go to the residence of the deceased. While the coroner did what he had to do, Gaynell would do an asset inventory of the deceased. As the coroner removed the body, Gaynell removed whatever valuables were in the home. It was her responsibility to make sure the valuables made it back to City Hall for proper disbursement.

With the collapse of the banks during the Depression, most people tended to keep cash on hand. So, not too surprisingly, most of the cash never found its way onto Gaynell's asset inventory sheet. Even if the deceased had a will, some of the items taken from the home were never returned to the next of kin.

It was during that time that Gaynell came to know Ben Brown, the man who, for years, served as the coroner for Los Angeles County and the man who would oversee the autopsies of Bugsy Siegel, Betty Ann MacDonald, and Robert MacDonald, some fourteen years later.

Shaw's administration had given the coroner's office the green light to be grave robbers, just so long as the mayor, his brother Joe, and their friends got their share. The relationship Gaynell had with the coroner's office during the mid-'30s was critical to the events that would happen in the mid-1940s. By working for Shaw, Gaynell was a first-hand witness to the corruption and graft for which Shaw's administration was infamous.

It is documented in the newspapers of the time that Shaw's group used its administrative powers to promote rank-and-file police officers to higher positions in the Los Angeles Police Department by providing answers to civil service tests. It is also recorded that, in addition to the LAPD and the coroner's office, Shaw's administration was able to influence the staffing of the district attorney's office.

By witnessing the intimate workings of the Shaw spoils systems, Gaynell knew which street officers became watch commanders, then sergeants, and then lieutenants as a result of a manipulated test score. She knew which young attorneys became assistant district attorneys due to the assistance of Joe Shaw, the mayor's brother, who sold civil service exams, and she took notice when various city politicians or prominent citizens met with the mayor and left with handfuls of jewelry or cash, taken from those who had passed away. The fact of the matter was that Gaynell Rockwell noticed a great many things during her time with the mayor, and by doing so had put herself into a position to be a very powerful woman, should she choose to be one.

Chapter Ten
Gaynell's Ticket to the Big Show

Ralph Applegate was born on his family's farm in Huntington, Indiana, on September 30, 1880. He was a hard worker all of his life, so it wasn't any surprise that his work ethic allowed him to make a small fortune in his chosen field of endeavor—mining! He moved to California in 1910 and found success uncapping the earthly riches of silver and gold offered by the Sierra Mountains.

Mining was hard work, especially with the hands-on approach that Applegate liked, but as Ralph got older, he looked to open other doors of opportunity. By the late 1920s, Ralph was in his forties. While the idea of working hard with his body appealed to him, the Hoosier native had decided to trade his pick and shovel in for a suit and tie. After making his fortune in mining, he shifted careers and had become an investment banker.

While many people lost everything they had when the stock market crashed in 1929, Applegate kept his finances strong. His reputation for being smart with money allowed him to develop a very extensive client base of people in the financial know.

Ralph was making a great deal of money doing what he was doing, but in many ways, he hated the hustle and bustle of the big city. He was a man who needed to be outside. He needed the sun, the sky, and Mother Nature around him. She gave him a rebirth every time he experienced the quiet splendor of an early morning or the beauty of a sunset. So in the late '20s, Ralph Applegate purchased a cabin in Bridgeport, California, a mountain community north of Los Angeles.

The smell of the trees and the crisp mountain air allowed Ralph to escape the craziness of the big city and proved to be an excellent location for him to relax. Upon arriving in Bridgeport, Applegate settled into his five-bedroom log cabin and took to heart the solace offered by the beauty of the Sierra Mountains.

Bridgeport gave birth to a Ralph Applegate tradition. Every Saturday morning, he would rise early, throw on a pair of light gray overalls, and leave Los Angeles for the small desert town of Mojave, where he would stop for breakfast and visit with other Saturday-morning travelers.

Applegate was a friendly man whose demeanor, combined with the premature whitening of his hair, gave him a happy-go-lucky grandfatherly persona. Nicknamed the "Gray Ghost of the Desert" by the Mojave locals, he found the people of that small desert town to be genuine and unpretentious, as they did him.

"Ralph was living an existence he hated," Gaynell once said. "His weekend junkets to Mojave were his only joy."

The fact was Applegate was just going through the motions of life. His job was mundane for him, his marriage to his wife of twenty years was dying, and there was absolutely no spark in his life. His life had no passion, no love, and no lust. Gaynell Rockwell changed all that.

* * * * *

"I met Ralph in City Hall," Gaynell once said. "I had been in a meeting with Franklin and Joe Shaw and had just left the mayor's office when I literally ran right into Ralph as he was coming around a corner."

Gaynell saw many things she liked about Ralph Applegate. Although an older gentleman, he was handsome, wealthy, and socially connected. Instantly, she recognized that Ralph Applegate could give her a social pedigree, the one thing she could never achieve on her own. Gaynell's association with Dragna and Shaw may have allowed her to secure her financial standing, but it had done nothing for her social status. Dragna was a mobster, Shaw, a corrupt politician. Applegate, on the other hand, was a respected businessman. Having been a member of the Breakfast Club since the early '20s, his list of associates included newspaper publishers, chancellors of universities, oil tycoons, and movie stars.

Ralph Applegate was the most intriguing man Gaynell Rockwell had ever met. It took her only a short period of time to conclude that if she could attach herself to him, her entry into Southern California's Upper-Class Society would be assured.

There was only one glitch. Ralph Applegate was a married man, a fact that, while a bit troublesome, mattered little to Gaynell. Once she discovered his marriage was on the rocks, she was like a shark with the scent of blood in the water.

"I was instantly attracted to Ralph," Gaynell once said. "He was a distinguished-looking man, with a warm personality, a sharp wit, and the ability to make me laugh. It didn't hurt that he was rich, too."

Gaynell saw Ralph as her deliverer and as a means for her to get to the "big show." There was another problem, however. She was in love with Nick Moretta. While Applegate offered Gaynell the things in life she craved—greater wealth, social status, and powerful connections, Nick was the love of her life.

Nick had been a father figure for Gaynell's two children, had been with her through the horrors of Renny's death, and he had brought her into Jack Dragna's circle of influence. Yet, for all he offered, he could never give her what she wanted more than anything—entry into the blue-blood world of Southern California's aristocratic society. Ralph Applegate could. There was nothing to think about. Gaynell knew she had to marry Ralph Applegate.

"When Gaynell told Nick she was going to pursue Ralph, Nick gave her his blessing," Marion Clark-Hull stated. "Nick knew if Gaynell married Ralph, it would open the door to a whole new world for both of them. She would never leave Nick. He knew it, and she knew it. They would still have their relationship; they would have to be more discreet about it.

* * * * *

Franklin Shaw asked Ralph Applegate to attend a social function at the home of Archibald A. MacDonald. "Archie" was a wealthy Southern California businessman who was throwing a party for Howard Hughes, America's most famous movie-maker and aviator.

That evening, Gaynell accompanied the mayor to the party. Archibald MacDonald provided Shaw with the opportunity to invite four guests, so in addition to Gaynell, the mayor requested that his brother, Joe, and his good friend, Ralph Applegate, attend the function as well.

As the evening progressed, the mayor and his brother eventually excused themselves, thereby leaving Gaynell and Applegate alone at the party. It didn't take Gaynell long to sense that Ralph Applegate was a man susceptible to the sexually-charged flirtations of a woman twenty years his junior.

As the champagne flowed and the evening progressed, Gaynell came to learn Applegate's entire life story. She also discovered that Ralph Applegate was sharp, witty, intelligent, and very dignified. Ralph and Gaynell exchanged stories. They became oblivious to those around them. Nothing seemed to matter to them except each other.

"It was like we were teenagers at the prom," Gaynell said in recalling the evening. "I was nervous at first, but by the end of the night, things had progressed to the point where we were very comfortable with each other."

When Applegate asked Gaynell if he could take her home, Gaynell said yes. Gaynell had never been one to hesitate about using her body as a means to obtain the things in life she desired. Having sex with Ralph that night was a given.

Applegate came alive. After meeting Gaynell, his outlook on life seemed to change completely. He and Gaynell were spending more and more time together, and Ralph was once again in love—a feeling that he had not experienced in some time.

Within a few months, Applegate filed for divorce from his wife of twenty years. Mrs. Applegate agreed to take twenty-five percent of Ralph's financial empire, making the divorce settlement an extremely amicable matter. He later discovered his wife had been having an affair of her own, which explained the civility of their breakup and her eagerness to settle the divorce quickly.

Not long after the final divorce papers were in, Ralph and Gaynell made a jaunt to Reno, Nevada, where they became Mr. and Mrs. Ralph Applegate. Gaynell's association with Shaw had allowed her to wiggle free of the economic hardships created by Renny's death. Her marriage to Applegate catapulted her into a world she'd never dreamed possible. Her ship had arrived, and she was now a member of Southern California's social elite. Gaynell had life on Easy Street…or so she thought.

* * * * *

Spring 1938

Gaynell had found what she was looking for and her days of hustling were over. She had left Shaw's fold and was now the wife of a millionaire. The timing of her separation from Shaw's empire could not have been any better.

The mayor's administration had been under the watchful eye of Clinton Clifford, a private crusader who was determined to expose the corruption associated with city politics. While Shaw's administration had always been suspected of engaging in illicit and illegal activities, no one could ever prove anyone in the mayor's office was conducting said activities. Clifford was determined to change that.

He hired former Los Angeles police officer Harry Raymond to dig up dirt on Shaw and his cronies. Raymond, who'd lost his job via the Carl Jacobson scandal, had a grudge against the City of Los Angeles. However, despite doing everything in his power to uncover something shocking and sensational, his investigation proved unspectacular.

Then someone planted a bomb in Harry's car, trying to blow up the private investigator. The primary rule of crime in Los Angeles had been violated. Dirty laundry had been aired in public.

The blunder left Raymond severely wounded. Yet, despite his suffering from broken bones, internal bleeding, and the presence of scrap-metal wounds, Harry was able to assist in the police investigation that eventually linked the attack to Shaw's administration, and specifically to Earle Kynette, a member of the Los Angeles Police Department.

The citizens of Los Angeles were forced to acknowledge that it was time to take a closer look at the allegations made against the mayor's office. A recall election was held, and he was voted out of office.

On September 16, 1938, Fletcher Bowron was elected mayor of Los Angeles. Within the first year of his term, James Davis was out as the chief of police, and over fifty ranking officers of the Los

Angeles Police Department were fired or had resigned from their positions.

* * * * *

Ralph Applegate was driven by an enormous desire to be successful, while at the same time having the good sense to enjoy life's simple offerings. In many ways, Ralph and Renny were frightfully similar. Both were strong and sensitive. Both were able to use their bodies to make a living—Renny in construction and Ralph in mining. Both were able to appreciate the beauty of a sunset, the sound of a bird's song, and the smell of the ocean breeze off the water, and both had been in love with Gaynell. Sadly, Gaynell never shared the same philosophy that Renny and Ralph had come to embrace.

As the '30s came to an end, everything was in place to assure Gaynell a happy and fortuitous life. The two Rockwell children—Bob, aged nineteen, and Betty Ann, aged seventeen—had completely accepted their stepfather. Ralph adored Gaynell. Bob had enrolled at the University of Southern California, and Betty Ann had become a student at an exclusive girls' school. Things could not have been much better.

"Gaynell always thought that once she achieved wealth and social status, she would be happy," Marion Clark-Hull stated. "She was wrong.

"Even though she had married Ralph, her heart belonged to Nick. In many ways, it always had. After Gaynell had moved into Ralph's home in Los Angeles, in 1938, Nick was still a fixture at our house. He was part of the family.

"We all knew Gaynell and Nick were seeing each other, even after Gaynell had married Ralph. It was sad, really, because Ralph was such a good man. My father used to rip into both Gaynell and Nick, but it didn't matter. The next day, Nick would be back at the house, either cooking with my mother in the kitchen or doing some type of work in the yard for my father.

"Eventually, Gaynell began to feel guilty about her affair with Nick. She and Mom had this long conversation, one night. They must have smoked four packs of cigarettes and gone through three pots of coffee."

Gaynell knew that divorcing Ralph would mean she would have to make do with a little less money. But unlike Ralph's first wife, Gaynell would seek half his finances in the divorce settlement.

"I always held hope, deep down, that Gaynell's motive for divorcing Ralph wasn't about money," Marion continued. "I felt Gaynell finally realized she had everything in life she had craved—money, wealth, and power—yet she didn't have the one thing she needed, which was love. By the end of her conversation with my mother, Gaynell had decided she was going to divorce Ralph and marry Nick. She wanted love. She wanted Nick.

"Gaynell and Ralph had made plans to get away to Bridgeport after the family picnic on the Fourth of July. Gaynell thought that if she broke the news to Ralph there, he would already be in the one place in the world that made him happy and maybe, just maybe, being among the things he loved the most would make Gaynell's announcement easier to accept."

* * * * *

July 1940

"One of the Rockwell family traditions was a Fourth of July barbecue," Marion Clark-Hull recalled. "The event was usually held at Huntington Beach, and always brought the entire family together for the day.

"Early in the morning, the men picked out our spot on the sand, dug a deep pit, began a fire, and then started to 'deep pit barbecue' a whole pig. The process took about twelve hours, so arriving before sunrise was critical if we were going to eat before sunset. The women of the family prepared for the day with an early morning of cooking at my mom's house, ensuring the Fourth was a festive event.

"I remember the Fourth of July 1940 like it was yesterday. The Fourth fell on a Thursday, that year. I was fifteen, Betty Ann seventeen, and the last thing we wanted to do was get up at four o'clock in the morning, spend hours in the kitchen cooking, and then go to the beach and spend the rest of the day with our families. At least, that was the front we put on.

"Betty Ann and I put on a ruse that we didn't like doing the family thing. Truth be known, we both loved the family tradition of the beach barbecues. We both liked to eat, and the feasting that took place on the Fourth of July was to die for: potato salad, macaroni salad, deviled eggs, fried chicken, freshly-squeezed lemonade, and a bevy of desserts were snacked on throughout the day. At night, after the pig was pulled from the pit, we feasted on barbecued pork sandwiches, baked beans, roasted corn-on-the-cob, and baked potatoes with all the trimmings.

"As Betty Ann and I walked along the beach that day, we talked girl talk. We laughed, and we daydreamed. I also recall that that was the first time I noticed boys—specifically, how their heads turned as we walked by them. I was smart enough to know the boys were not looking at me. I was a flat-chested fifteen-year-old. Betty Ann, on the other hand, had become a very attractive girl.

"She had been attending an exclusive girls' school, and I could tell, simply by the way she carried herself, that she was transforming into womanhood. Her mannerisms, the way she talked, the way she walked, everything about her was changing. She was becoming a lady.

"Betty Ann had watched over me my whole life. She took care of me, she picked on me, she pampered me, she spoiled me, and for as long as I can remember, she loved me. Walking along the beach that day, I came to understand this. I don't know why, but I did. Nothing was said, no sentimental words exchanged, nothing I can pinpoint as being a defining moment in our relationship. I simply came to understand that the bond Betty Ann and I had was special. It was a wonderful feeling."

* * * * *

"On the morning of July 5th," Marion continued, "Betty Ann and I were going to go to the University of San Diego, for a visit with a friend of hers who was a student there. When Betty Ann arrived at the house, she came with a car full of gifts. My fifteenth birthday was just a few weeks away, and Betty Ann had decided to celebrate early. She brought boxes of clothes into our house. It seemed as if she was trying to fill my entire closet. It was the most incredible thing I had ever experienced.

"Once all the clothes were scattered across my room, Betty Ann insisted that we have a teaching moment so I could learn how to match cloth and colors. She always had an eagerness to share with me what she had learned at charm school. I always chuckled at her attempts to make me into a proper lady.

"Betty Ann always started out trying to take our lessons seriously. From posture to dining etiquette, to proper introductory expressions, she tried to teach it all to me. It was to no avail. She could never make it through one of our charm school lessons without bursting into laughter. She would always let out an explosive giggle, which would, of course, cause me to lose the business-like mood of the moment.

"That Fourth of July weekend was one of the best times I ever had. Sadly, however, things went downhill from there, and it was probably the last time our family experienced any kind of joy."

* * * * *

Gaynell and Ralph were supposed to leave for Bridgeport on July 5th. However, after an enormous fight soured the mood, the trip was canceled, and Gaynell and Ralph spent the weekend not talking to each other.

On July 8th, Ralph decided he was going to go to Bridgeport by himself. He got up early in the morning, packed a bag, loaded his car, and left Gaynell a note saying he would be at the cabin for the week.

As Ralph headed down the road, en route to his favorite café in the Mojave Desert, his mind was spinning. When he arrived at the eatery on a Monday morning, even the regulars were confused. Ralph being there during the week was uncommon.

Breakfast came and went. After several cups of coffee, and a few hours of reflection, Ralph ordered lunch. His cup was kept full through the afternoon. Those in the café could see that his mind was racing as quickly as the traffic on the highway outside, yet they respected the Gray Ghost of the Desert's right to privacy and left him alone.

Ralph loved Gaynell, but she had grown distant in the previous few months. Being twenty years older than she, he'd expected they would have some issues, but nothing they couldn't handle if they only worked together.

The lunch menus were switched over to the dinner menus, and as the night crew replaced the afternoon workers, Ralph decided to return to Los Angeles. He left his favorite café that day without saying goodbye to a single soul. He merely paid his $4.25 tab by leaving a twenty-dollar bill on the table.

When he pulled into his house at 815 South Hudson, he saw that Gaynell's car was in the driveway and the convertible was gone. That meant that Gaynell was home; Betty Ann was not. Ralph parked his car, walked up the drive, and entered his home.

After looking through the living room and kitchen, he proceeded upstairs. He heard noises coming from the bedroom. When he opened the door, he discovered Gaynell and Nick making love.

"There was a brief exchange of words," Gaynell once admitted. "Understandably, Ralph was enraged when he left. He slammed the bedroom door shut, and then stormed from the house. By the time I threw something on and ran downstairs, he had backed the car out of the driveway and was racing toward Wilshire Boulevard. I went to bed that night figuring he had gone to Bridgeport and was confident that, when he returned, he would be the one asking for the divorce."

* * * * *

The newspaper caption read *AUTO DEMOLISHED*. The article went on to say:

> "Crashing head-on into a west-bound 'R' street car piloted by Motorman R.E. Meyers, who escaped injury, the unidentified victim's machine was demolished and he was killed instantly. The machine, registered to Gaynell Applegate, 815 South Hudson Avenue, was jammed so tightly beneath the streetcar that an emergency truck and another streetcar were necessary to disentangle it."

Firemen and police needed almost five hours to remove Ralph's body from the mangled wreckage. Later, it was officially determined that the car had probably malfunctioned.

"It was about 1:30 A.M. when the police arrived at Gaynell's house," Marion Clark-Hull recalled. "Mom got the call from Gaynell shortly thereafter.

"'Good God Almighty,' Gaynell cried into the phone. 'Flossy come quickly. Ralph's been killed in a car accident.'

"The night Ralph died seemed to be the point in Gaynell's life where things began to unravel," Marion continued. "Even though Gaynell inherited Applegate's fortune, she also inherited the guilt associated with the realization that Ralph's death was probably suicide and her deeds had contributed to his death. It was something that weighed on her conscience for the rest of her life."

Chapter Eleven

Howard Hughes—Father and Son

Howard Hughes, Sr., was the second of four children born to Felix and Jean Hughes. He was born in Lancaster, Missouri, in 1869.

Felix Hughes was a school superintendent who eventually became a powerful lawyer. The elder Hughes would have liked Howard to have attended an Ivy League school, but Howard was a bit of a maverick and chose to put his energy into mining. Despite his enthusiasm for mining, Hughes made a poor living as a miner, so in January of 1901, when oil was discovered in Texas, Hughes, like thousands of others, caught oil fever and set out to make his fortune.

In 1905, Hughes met and later married Allene Gano. In December of 1905, the couple had their first and only child; Howard Hughes, Jr. Life for the Hughes family was a struggle, as Hughes bounced from job to job. For a while, it didn't appear as if he was going to have any more success chasing oil than he had digging in the dirt.

In 1909, Hughes took his wife and child to Louisiana, where it was speculated that the next significant oil find would be made. To pay the bills and support his family, he found work delivering the mail and upholding the law. He also fell into a partnership with Walter Sharp, an oilman from Texas.

Sharp seemed to have a knack for finding the black, bubbling crude. If nothing else, he and Hughes shared a passion for the oil business, so the union seemed to be a win-win situation. Both men knew there was oil beneath the soil, but getting to it had become a difficult, if not impossible, task. The drilling technology of the time allowed for only a superficial penetration of the earth's surface, which made getting to the oil a constant source of frustration.

One night, in a Louisiana bar, Hughes met Granville Humason, who was trying to get someone to pay him for a crude, wooden mock-up of a drill bit that he had designed. Hughes looked at the device, instantly realized that the concept was revolutionary, and offered the man $150.00 for the rights to the bit design. Humason accepted Hughes' offer and bought the bar patrons a round of drinks out of the earnings from his design. Hughes later took the bit, modified it, and within a few months, he and his partner, Walter Sharp, began mass production of the device. However, instead of selling the bits outright, the Sharp-Hughes Tool Company leased the bits to oil companies for a yearly fee. At $30,000.00 a year, per bit, the decision to lease the bits and not sell them outright proved to be nothing short of genius.

On November 28, 1912, Walter Sharp died suddenly at the age of forty-two. His wife, Estelle, inherited half-ownership in the tool company. Less than two years later, she sold her shares to a third party. That person eventually sold his shares in the company to Howard Hughes, Sr., thereby giving birth to the Hughes Tool Company in February of 1915. New gushers were springing up across the Texas plains as rapidly as Hughes bits could be delivered, and Big Howard's bank accounts were growing almost as fast as oil was spurting from the ground.

* * * * *

Howard Hughes, Jr., was born on Christmas Eve 1905, in Houston, Texas. As a youngster, Junior was never extremely social but did enjoy working with his hands. He loved to tinker with mechanical things, and he had a passion for mathematics.

Big Howard wanted his son to have the best education possible, so in the fall of 1919, the younger Hughes was sent to the Fressenden Boarding School in Massachusetts. Despite the wishes of his father, Howard failed to catch on "academic fire," and was taken out of school less than a year later.

In the early '20s, the Hughes family began to frequent California, and by the fall of 1921, the Hughes Tool Company had opened a branch office in Los Angeles. Still hoping to give his son a formal education, in September of 1921, Big Howard enrolled Howard in the Thacher School, an exclusive private school located in Ojai, California.

Howard's studies went very well his first semester, and for a brief period of time, he seemed to truly enjoy his commitment to academics. However, in March of 1922, the Hughes' world was shattered when Allene Hughes died unexpectedly during a routine operation. Howard, just sixteen years old when his mother passed away, was utterly devastated by the news of her passing. He withdrew from Thacher and returned to Texas.

In September of 1922, Hughes returned to Thacher, but just before to Christmas of that year withdrew again. In the spring of 1923, he was enrolled, at least on paper, at the California Institute of Technology in Pasadena, where records show he never attended classes. In the fall of 1923, he enrolled at the Rice Institute in Texas. Once again, however, Hughes dropped out of school before completing any coursework. On the surface, Howard Hughes seemed to be a young man without direction or the ability to complete simple tasks, such as completing an education; this was far from the case.

Young Howard's life changed forever on January 14, 1924, when his father, Big Howard, died of a heart attack. The elder Hughes' death left Howard, at the age of nineteen, a seventy-five-percent shareholder in one of the world's most prosperous businesses. By Texas law, Howard could not take legal control of the Hughes Tool Company until he was twenty-one. This statute, however, did not dissuade him from attempting to acquire complete control of the company. In May of 1924, Hughes paid his grandparents and Uncle Rupert $325,000.00 for the outstanding twenty-five percent of the Hughes Tool Company.

With the help of Hughes Tool Company top aides, Hughes challenged Texas state law prohibiting minors from controlling businesses and making business decisions. On December 26, 1924, Howard Hughes gained control of his life and the Hughes Tool Company, when a Texas Court declared him of age and unbound by the rules governing minors.

On June 1, 1925, Hughes married Ella Rice in Houston, Texas. His marriage was not driven by love, but rather by image. Hughes was making grand plans to move to California and take Hollywood by storm. Having a wife on his arm was seen, by Howard, as a symbol of maturity and a necessary component of the image of adulthood.

The union of Howard Hughes and Ella Rice had all the components of a storybook tale. Howard and Ella were from Houston's new aristocratic society. Hughes was the son of an oil tycoon, while Ella was the daughter of David Rice, who was the brother of William Rice, founder of the Rice Institute.

"Howard felt he needed a wife," Gaynell once said. "Arranged marriages were still commonplace in the South, so after some bargaining, Hughes took a bride, and in the fall of 1925, Howard and his new wife relocated to sunny Southern California."

Howard Hughes was never going to be a businessman. He had too much imagination and too much energy to sit behind a desk and handle the daily tasks of overseeing invoices and transportation requests and reviewing payroll sheets. Rupert Hughes was probably more responsible for Howard's interest in Hollywood than anything. Howard had been visiting Uncle Rupert in California off and on since he was a small child, and without question, Rupert had a tremendous influence on him. Howard came to Hollywood with a pocket full of money, but no experience in the film industry, a combination that would prove costly, but only on a small scale.

While golfing one afternoon, he discovered one of his golfing associates; a man named Ralph Graves had written a screenplay and was hoping to have it made into a movie. As it was, Hughes was hoping to produce a movie. The two men shook hands; Hughes paid for the cost of the film up front and watched from the wings as Graves made Howard Hughes' first film.

Within a few months, the film, Swell Hogan, was finished. It cost twice as much as projected and was horrible. The movie never saw a theater, and Hughes never gave up control of a motion picture again.

Howard formed Caddo Productions, and his next film, *Everybody's Acting*, made him a profit. *Two Arabian Nights*, starring William Boyd (later of *Hopalong Cassidy* fame), followed. He was right in the mix of things for that picture, taking control of every aspect of the production, which drove the cast and crew crazy but made

him very happy. The film won Lewis Milestone, the credited director, an Academy Award.

If Howard Hughes had any outlet at all from the rigors of his
filmmaking career, it had to be flying. As a small child, he and his
father had taken a ride in a seaplane. The event hooked Howard
on the joy of flying, and he might have begun a career in aviation
earlier in his life had his father allowed him. Flying was too dangerous in the eyes of the elder Hughes, so only after the passing of his
father did Howard, Jr. begin taking flying lessons to satisfy one of
the true loves of his life.

In May of 1927, much of the world was captivated by the flight
of Charles Lindbergh, Howard Hughes included. Lindbergh's
achievement seemed to be a significant turning point in Howard's life, as his next film, *Hell's Angels*, paid homage to the pilots of
World War I. The movie starred Ben Lyon and launched the career
of Jean Harlow, who had only a small part in the picture.

Hughes began filming *Hell's Angels* in October of 1927. By January of 1928, he'd received his pilot's license, and as the twenties were
coming to an end, he was spending all of his time making films and
flying, a situation that didn't sit well with Howard's wife, Ella.

As Howard's commitment to his professional life began to take
more and more of his time, Ella Hughes decided to separate from
her husband. She did this in October of 1928 and returned to Texas. Ella probably would have tried to save the marriage, but there
was little reason to do so. Howard was a man possessed by two
careers and had no time for a wife. When Ella divorced Hughes in
December of 1929, Howard Hughes probably gave a slight sigh of
relief. He had taken a wife for all the wrong reasons, and in Hughes'
eyes, Ella was better off without him.

The cast and crew of *Hell's Angels* probably felt that they would
have been better off without Howard Hughes, as well. The twenty-
six-year-old producer insisted on being in control of every aspect of
the film. In the end, however, he produced one of the most incredible flying films ever to come out of Hollywoodland and was finally
given his due as a moviemaker.

As the majority of the country was suffering from the effects of
the Great Depression, Howard Hughes was on top of the world.

His social circle was expanding, and now included the likes of Hollywood legends Irving Thalberg, Louis B. Mayer, Douglas Fairbanks, Jack Warner, and newspaper publishers Harry Chandler of the *Los Angeles Times* and William Randolph Hearst.

He was also gaining a reputation as a ladies' man. Over the years, the women in Howard Hughes' life would read like a "Who's Who" of Hollywood film legends: Billie Dove, Bette Davis, Ida Lupino, Rita Hayworth, Lana Turner, Ginger Rogers, Mary Pickford, Terry Moore, Ava Gardner, Marilyn Monroe, and a bevy of young starlets, who may or may not have ever made it to the silver screen.

"Howard Hughes was rumored to have slept with almost every woman in Hollywood," Gaynell Rockwell once said with a chuckle. "I have no doubt some of the rumors of Howard's conquests were true. Equally, I have no doubt some of his rumored conquests were not true."

With regard to Howard Hughes' relationships, however, one thing seems to be clear: of all the women in Howard's life, one seemed to capture his heart more than any other—Katharine Hepburn.

"Our family didn't come to know Howard Hughes until the early '40s," Gaynell continued. "In 1941, I was at a Christmas party given by Archie MacDonald, where Hughes was in attendance. I was standing next to our host when Hughes approached and, with a giggle, said to Archie that he had received a call from Hepburn wishing him a merry Christmas. By the way, Howard's eyes were lit up, and by the genuine smile on his face, I could tell Howard truly loved her."

Katharine Hepburn did seem to have Howard Hughes' heart, in part probably because, unlike so many of the other women in Hughes life, she was a great deal like Howard. Both Hughes and Hepburn had somewhat private personalities, although their bold, strong inner demeanors allowed each to be powerful and controlling, when necessary. Both had a wit that very few people understood. And both shared a zest for life that too few people share.

"If there was ever a woman that Howard Hughes could have settled down with, and been happy with, it probably was Katharine Hepburn," Gaynell once stated. "Hughes asked Hepburn to marry him, but she laughed him off. Like Hughes, Hepburn knew she wasn't the marrying type. She was, however, a woman of commitment, and while she was with Howard, she was committed to him heart, and soul."

Later, Hepburn would commit herself to Spencer Tracy and remain true to her famous screen partner for the remainder of his life. Hughes, on the other hand, never again experienced much of a meaningful relationship. From his marriage to Ella Rice to his marriage to Jean Peters, Howard Hughes' relationships with women seemed to always be a bit bizarre. Maybe this was one reason Howard Hughes chose to focus his attention on the other loves in his life, film, and flight.

While Howard Hughes never achieved success in a monogamous relationship, he did go on to have a great career in film. *Scarface* (1932), inspired by the career of Al Capone, was directed by Howard Hawks and starred Paul Muni, George Raft, Ann Dvorak, Karen Morley, and Boris Karloff. It, along with *Little Caesar* (1930) with Edward G. Robinson and *Public Enemy* (1931), defined the American gangster film. *The Outlaw* (1943) introduced Jane Russell to the world and is still considered one of the most controversial films of its day, due to the emphasis credited director Hughes placed on Miss Russell's breasts throughout the film.

* * * * *

By 1932, the concept of flight had completely captivated Hughes. Initially, he got his foot in the door of the aviation business due to his making of *Hell's Angels*, since with that production, he had purchased a number of planes that he stored in a leased Lockheed aircraft hangar.

There was something about the sky that Hughes loved. Maybe it was the freedom he felt when he was alone in the sky. Or perhaps it was the way the blood pumped through his veins during the thrill of a take-off. Whatever it was, Hughes had loved flying since his father had paid for that ten-dollar ride and in 1932, Hughes founded the Hughes Aircraft Company in Glendale, California.

Through the 1930s, Hughes was involved in the development of many successful planes and personally served as a test pilot on many of the company's prototypes. During World War II, Hughes

Aircraft was granted a number of contracts through the Defense Plant Corporation, an offshoot of President Roosevelt's Reconstruction Finance Corporation. This arrangement netted Hughes millions. It was this work, as a defense contractor during World War II, which sparked a Senate War Investigating Committee probe of Hughes Aircraft, in August of 1947.

While the Senate subcommittee investigating Hughes Aircraft explored numerous allegations against Hughes, the company's work on the Hercules HK-I, the "Spruce Goose," seemed to be the smoking gun that proved to the subcommittee members that Hughes had bilked the American people out of millions of dollars. After all, there was no way that an aircraft whose body and wings were made completely of wood, which was 750 feet long, one hundred feet high, and 250 feet wide, could ever fly. Right? Amazingly, less than three months later, Hughes gained worldwide recognition when the plane took to the air, thereby ending the Senate investigation.

* * * * *

While Hughes' rise to power was one of the most dramatic in American history, Hughes the man is often misunderstood. Without question, Howard Hughes was one of the most influential men of the twentieth century, and in many ways, so, too, were the men of his inner circle.

"The stereotype of Howard Hughes was that he was cold, uncaring, all business-like," Gaynell once said. "The truth of the matter was that Howard Hughes was generous, warm, and very caring. He certainly had his business persona, but due to his meteoric rise as an oilman, filmmaker, and aviator, few people had time to focus on Howard the person, which was too bad because he was a very good man."

Chapter Twelve
The Guardian of the Empire

Archibald Angus MacDonald was born to Angus John Mac-Donald and Frances Mary McHugh in Minneapolis, Minnesota, on February 28, 1893. By the time "Archie" MacDonald reached his late teens, he had married Ellen "Ella" Crosbie. Archie and his new bride moved to Houston, Texas, to pursue the dream of striking it rich in the oil business. Initially, life for the MacDonald's was a struggle. The couple lived in a small, one-bedroom, dirt-floor shack, and often wondered where their next meal was coming from.

"It had gotten to the point where I was going to give up on my dream and get into the retail business," Archie once said. "As fate had it, however, I met Howard Hughes, Sr. Within a few months, I learned how important it was to be in the right place at the right time. I came aboard the Sharp-Hughes Tool Company just before Howard's bit design was used on the Goose Creek well. Talk about being lucky."

When the bit worked to perfection and opened up a well once thought unreachable, life for Hughes and MacDonald changed dramatically. The Sharp-Hughes Tool Company became the Hughes Tool Company, and Archie MacDonald was appointed as an executive for the Board of Directors. Life for MacDonald was never going to be the same.

When Hughes decided to expand the company's operation to California, Archie was dispatched to launch a variety of subsidiary companies for disbursing Hughes Oil manufacturing products. His first job in Southern California was to keep the books for the Associated Supply Company, a satellite business of Hughes' growing empire.

In 1917, MacDonald bounced to the Lucey Manufacturing Company, where his "official" title was that of "Clerk." The following year, he assumed the title of salesman for Lucey, and in 1919, became the assistant manager of Lucey.

"I never knew why Archie was tied with all those companies," Gaynell once said. "As far as I knew, he had been associated with Hughes since the early days. The whole Hughes thing was so clandestine. The money the company was making was staggering. Hughes had hundreds of little companies all around the world, and I have no doubt Archie was involved, in name and paycheck only, in a number of those Hughes ventures. Even though Archie was off the books with Tool Co by the mid-1930's, he worked for, and with, Howard through the late 1940's."

In 1921, Ella gave birth to a son, Robert. It was also about this time that Archie's relationship with Howard Hughes, Jr. began to blossom, as well. While Howard Hughes, Jr.'s family contact in California was his uncle, Rupert Hughes, it was Archie who was charged by Big Howard with looking out for Junior. MacDonald and Howard began to form a friendship that would last a lifetime.

Gaynell: "I think it was probably about this time that Ella became a bit resentful of her husband's commitment to Big Howard, Junior, and the Hughes Tool Company in general."

In the fall of 1923, MacDonald's loyalty to the Hughes family was rewarded when Big Howard appointed Archie general manager of the Hughes Tool Company's branch office in Los Angeles. At the age of thirty, Archibald "Archie" MacDonald was a major player in the most prosperous company in the world.

* * * * *

By early 1924, Archie was working out of the Hughes Tool Company office in Los Angeles, California. The office, located at 2040 North Berendo, became the hub of the Hughes West Coast operations.

As a consequence of Archie's position, Ellea was thrust into the position of playing hostess for a variety of Hughes-related functions. "The MacDonald home became the entertainment center for the Hughes Tool Company," Gaynell once said. "Christmas parties, business meetings, anniversary celebrations—the MacDonald's were expected to represent Big Howard and his interests whenever someone of importance visited California. Events happened almost weekly."

Whenever Big Howard or Junior came to town, Archie was the one who took care of all the arrangements. As Archie began to spend more and more time with Howard, Jr., it became apparent to MacDonald that Big Howard's brilliance had been passed along to his only child. He saw a style in Junior that he liked—an intelligent, charismatic teenager who, one day, would have the world in the palm of his hand.

"My relationship with the Hughes Tool Company allowed me to achieve wealth, power, influence, and social status," MacDonald once stated. "After Big Howard died, the stability of the Hughes Tool Company was in question. When Rupert Hughes made the suggestion he be named Howard's guardian, all of us associated with Hughes Tool saw his overture as a threat to our livelihoods. As one of the executive members of the Board of Directors, I made it my personal mission to see that Howard gained control of the company.

"There were several hurdles that Howard had to overcome if he wanted to control Hughes Tool," Archie continued. "His relatives were the first obstacles. The Hughes family was fearful that Howard was merely interested in taking over the Tool Company to finance a Hollywood playboy lifestyle. In many respects, they were right, but nonetheless, everyone associated with Howard knew he was the right person to run his father's company.

"Due to the death of his mother, and Big Howard's failure to redo his will before his passing, Howard was entitled to seventy-five percent of the company when his father died. In April, we opened negotiations with Howard's family for the remaining twenty-five percent, and by May of 1924, an agreement was reached to compensate Howard's relatives $325,000 for their shares of the Hughes Tool Company.

"The second problem Howard encountered was Texas law," Archie went on. "The Disabilities as a Minor law prevented anyone under the age of twenty-one from entering into a binding contract. We saw a loophole in a statutory provision of the Texas Civil Code, however, and discovered that if minors could convince the court that they could handle their own affairs, they could be declared competent and, therefore, legally engage in binding agreements.

When the time came, Howard convinced the judge to approve his request for the removal of his status as a minor, and on December 26, 1924, Howard was declared competent to run his affairs."

Howard Hughes was very aware that Archibald MacDonald was critical in helping him take the steps necessary to gain complete control of his father's company. While Hughes recognized and rewarded MacDonald's loyalty, more importantly, he came to realize that Archie MacDonald was someone he could count on for the rest of his life.

* * * * *

Archie was one of the few people who knew Howard Hughes on a personal level. He saw first-hand the metamorphosis of Hughes from boy to man.

"By his late teens, Howard had transformed himself into a strapping young adult," Archie stated. "He had become a man who possessed the aggressiveness, tenacity, and instincts necessary to run a multi-million dollar business."

After Hughes had divorced his wife, Ella Rice, and become one of the most eligible bachelors in Hollywood, the young millionaire's life was placed under constant scrutiny. The gossip-hungry press reported every romance, personal indiscretion, or business deal Howard Hughes was supposedly involved with.

It became apparent that, if the Hughes Tool Company was going to continue to work effectively, keeping the happenings of Hughes' life out of the public eye was a necessity—a difficult task, to be sure. Hughes recognized his need to have someone troubleshoot potential problems that were surely going to arise from time to time, so he designated MacDonald to be the "guardian of the empire," a move which essentially gave birth to what became known as the "Hughes Secrecy Machine."

* * * * *

Archie's most famous cover-up was in regards to an accident Hughes had, in which the car he was driving struck and killed a pedestrian in July of 1936. Hughes, Pat DiCicco, and a lady friend had just finished having dinner and drinks at the Ambassador Hotel's Coconut Grove in Los Angeles.

DiCicco was a gangster and served as Charlie Luciano's liaison to the West Coast. He was also the former husband of Thelma Todd, the Hollywood comedienne who was later found dead in her car under very mysterious conditions. While some claim Todd's death was a suicide, more people believe she was murdered.

Regardless, DiCicco and Hughes were associates and enjoyed each other's company. Throughout the evening, the group indulged in a bottle or two of champagne, chatted about a few business items, and then said good-byes over "one last round" for the road.

Hughes and his lady friend left the hotel in Hughes' $16,500 Duesenberg convertible coupe. Fewer than a few miles from the hotel, while driving down Third Street in Los Angeles, Hughes struck Gabe S. Meyer, a fifty-nine-year-old salesman from Los Angeles, who died at the scene.

Details of the accident varied. At the scene, William Scott, a United Parcel Service (UPS) employee made a statement to the police. In essence, he told police that "the car driven by Hughes was traveling in front of him at a terrific rate of speed, and the deceased had been crossing the street within the streetcar safety zone area when struck by the Hughes vehicle."

Hughes was asked to make a statement at the scene but refused to answer any police questions. As a result, he was taken into custody, transported to the Wilshire Police Station, and booked on suspicion of violating Section 500 of the Vehicle Code, which is negligent homicide.

The first phone call Hughes made was to Archie MacDonald. By the mid-'30s, Archie was a master of damage control, and after assessing the potential consequences that could befall Howard, he developed a plan of attack designed to limit both public and political fallout.

Archie knew that if Hughes were convicted of vehicular homicide and assigned jail time, the Hughes Empire would be in danger of collapse—a scenario that could not occur.

With the evidence at hand, and more importantly, the testimony of the eyewitness, Scott, the prosecution had an open-and-shut case. Even though Los Angeles police officers and politicians were easily bribable, there was an outside factor with regard to this matter, the witness.

On Sunday, July 12, 1936, Archie MacDonald arranged to meet with Mr. Scott in a downtown Los Angeles office. After that meeting, William Scott was not seen by anyone, especially anyone associated with the District Attorney's office, until the day of the coroner's inquest, which was held on Wednesday, July 15, 1936.

To the astonishment of the prosecution, when Scott was called to take the stand and provide his testimony, his entire story had changed. Scott stated at the inquest that he was driving in front of the Hughes car and Mr. Meyer was not in the streetcar safety zone, but was, in fact, about twenty feet from it. Scott went on to state that Hughes was probably driving at no more than eighteen to twenty miles an hour when the accident occurred, and in his opinion, was driving in a safe manner.

At this point, prosecutors reminded Scott of the story he had given police the night of the accident. After patiently waiting for the prosecutor to read every word from the notepad, Scott calmly responded that officers at the scene must have misunderstood his statements that evening, and then assured the prosecutor and everyone attending the inquest that the sworn testimony he was giving was the true and accurate account of the event.

After Scott's testimony, Howard Hughes was brought to the stand to testify on his behalf. Hughes provided a detailed account of the evening, identical to that of Scott's. Hughes was a strong and powerful witness, who was able to explain the accident as a very unfortunate occurrence.

With the prosecution's prime witness aligning with the defense and supporting Hughes' testimony, the six-man jury took eighteen minutes before exonerating the driver in the accident of any wrong-doing. The district attorney had no grounds on which to charge Hughes with negligent homicide, and the case was closed.

* * * * *

Over the years, Howard Hughes provided MacDonald with many more opportunities to master his damage-control craft. There were innumerable starlets who needed to be hushed in regards to sexual encounters with Hughes, countless politicians who needed to be bribed, and a myriad of business deals that required the resourcefulness and special fix-it abilities of Archie MacDonald.

As a result of his experiences with Hughes, Archie came to learn every trick in the trade with regard to keeping secrets. Sadly, however, Archie's skills in the area of deception and concealment would one day have to be used to cover his own horrible family secret.

Chapter Thirteen
Bob MacDonald

B ob MacDonald was born to Archie and Ellea MacDonald on January 4, 1921. By the early 1920s, Archie was worth over one million dollars, so Bob was indeed born with a silver spoon in his mouth.

"If there was ever an argument made for the concept that a child is merely a product of his environment, Bob MacDonald could be the poster child for that concept," Gaynell once said. "Bob had a horrible childhood. His mother was as cold and callous a person as I have ever met. It also didn't help that both Ella and Archie used Howard Hughes' success as a barometer for their own children's achievements."

Marion: "I went with Betty Ann to several MacDonald family functions. In the eight years I had contact with Ella, I never saw her smile. She was the perfect example of how someone can have all the money in the world and still be a miserable human being. Archie, on the other hand, was one of the nicest people I'd ever met—a true gentleman in every sense of the word."

"There were probably several factors that led to Ella's bitterness toward life," Gaynell said. "She lived through some hard times when she first married Archie. Their house was a dirt-floored shack in Texas. Then, after Hughes struck oil, Ella discovered she had married a man who enjoyed his work more than he enjoyed being with his wife. But more than anything, she didn't like the fact that Archie was living in the shadow of Hughes and that, in everything but name, he was Hughes' twenty-four-hour-a-day servant."

Yet, at the forefront of Ella's hard-hearted attitude was the death of one of her children.

Gaynell: "An older brother of Bob's was killed in a motorcycle accident. It happened at a major intersection in downtown Los Angeles. There were many days when Bob and Betty Ann had to retrieve Ella from the scene of the accident. They would find her either sitting on the curb weeping or in the middle of the intersection crying hysterically.

"Although Bob always wanted to be there for his mother, he seemed to take the brunt of her bitterness toward her losing a child. There were many times when Ella's frustration with Bob would lead to her telling him that she wished it was he who had been killed in the accident."

Overcoming an uncaring, distant, cold mother was difficult enough, but Bob MacDonald also had another major obstacle in his life. He had to overcome the Hughes factor. Working for Howard Hughes did require Archie to be available seven days a week, twenty-four hours a day, and 365 days a year.

Gaynell: "I think Ella was probably concerned with Howard's playboy reputation. Archie spent a lot of time with Hughes, and who was to say if a Hughes stray didn't find her way into Archie's bed, or under or on top of his desk at work?

"It would have never happened. Archie MacDonald was a good man, committed to his wife, his family, and more often than not, his job. Unlike Howard, I doubt he had time for women.

"The bottom line was that when Archie was available, Ella wanted him to herself, and by the early 1930s, she made sure that what little time he had away from Hughes was going to be spent with her, even at the expense of her children. Betty Ann was told by Bob MacDonald that, because his father and mother were so busy tending to Hughes and the requirements of being associated with the Hughes Tool Company, he and his siblings were shipped off to boarding schools. Then, in the summer, Ella traditionally planned her and Archie's vacations, so the fact of the matter was that there was minimal contact for either Ella or Archie MacDonald with their children."

Marion: "I was always under the impression that Mr. and Mrs. MacDonald began their vacations a few days before the children were to return home from their boarding schools. The MacDonalds then returned a few days before the children were set to return to class in the fall. I heard Bob tell on several occasions how his parents were always gone when he was a child and how, if it were not for the hired help, he and his siblings would have had miserable summers."

While Archie MacDonald was seldom home, and probably did not get to spend as much time with his children as he would have liked, he cherished what time he did have with them.

"I only heard Bob MacDonald talk a few times about his childhood in a positive light," Gaynell once said. "Without question, Bob loved the time he spent with his father. Talking about Archie usually, put a glow on his face.

"One story Bob enjoyed sharing over and over again was in regards to an incident that happened at a big party held for members of the Hughes Tool Company, Hughes Aircraft, and a number of city and state officials. Ironically, due to my responsibilities with Mayor Shaw's office, I was at the party with Ralph, which was essentially our first date.

"Bob was just twelve years old. He had been told by Ella to stay in the house and not to interrupt the adult gathering. Well, Bob was a typical twelve-year-old, so there was no way he was going to make it through the entire night without going outside.

"As it turned out, Bob snuck down and began playing in the pond in the backyard. After discovering a rather large bullfrog, he had to share his find with his parents. He proudly approached Ella and displayed his new friend. Her reaction was not what he expected. Ella exploded in a fit of rage and embarrassment.

"After being scolded by his mother, Bob shuffled off toward the house. Archie, sensing his son's disappointment, walked with the boy and tried to use the mishap as a teaching moment. Howard Hughes spotted them and called them over. Once Bob came within Hughes' reach, Howard gave Bob a vigorous rubbing on his head, then shifted his attention to the frog.

"'Hey, great lookin' frog,' Hughes said to Bob.

"Howard's interest in the frog sparked Bob's enthusiasm for his find once again, but before he could expand on his discovery, Archie told him to return the frog to the pond and head inside the house as he was told to do by his mother. As Bob shuffled away, Howard said something to Archie, who in turn yelled out to his son. 'Hey,'

Archie said, 'Howard wants to take you to a picture show tomorrow. Do you want to go?'

"Bob's excitement could not be contained. He ran back to his father and Hughes and then stuck his hand out to Howard. There was only one problem. The frog was still firmly in Bob's grasp.

"Bob switched the frog to his left hand, wiped his right hand on his pants, then extended his right hand to Hughes again. Hughes chuckled as he took Bob's hand and shook it briskly.

"The joy Bob MacDonald received from that single childhood moment was amazing. No matter how many times he shared that story, the outcome was the same; Bob MacDonald loved that moment in his childhood. Unfortunately, that was about the only happy story Bob ever shared.

"Make no mistake, Archie had a good heart," Gaynell continued. "I always suspected that if he were put in a different profession, one where he made a living working nine to five, he would have been a man much like Renny Rockwell.

"Archie loved the beach. He loved to watch the sunrise and loved to watch the sunset. As Archie got older, and after the horrors that occurred later in our lives, he was the only one who was smart enough to take time for himself. Like me, I believe if Archie had to do it all over again, he would have given up the millions of dollars he made and been very content with being just an average Joe who was smart enough to enjoy life.

"Howard's success put an incredible amount of pressure on Bob," Gaynell went on. "Archie and Ella were constantly comparing the progress of their children's lives with that of Hughes."

"Howard was one of the most successful men in America," Archie once stated to Gaynell. "It was difficult for me not to hope Bob developed some of Howard's qualities."

"Archie was frequently frustrated by Bob's lack of motivation," Gaynell said. "I was present several times when Archie made remarks to Bob that let him know he wished Bob was more like Hughes."

Indeed, if one were to believe children are products of their environment, it isn't any wonder Bob MacDonald's life went down the path that it did. He was brought up in a home with a cold-hearted mother, a father who was never there and was constantly being compared to possibly the most successful human being on the face of the Earth.

Renny and Betty Ann Rockwell – Mid 1920's.

Due to Renny Rockwell's association with Jack Dragna, construction contracts awarded by the City of Los Angeles allowed Rockwell construction to prosper. (Renny, Gaynell, Betty Ann and Bob Rockwell)

The "Official" 1941 wedding picture. Betty Ann was already pregnant and showing – a no-no for a Catholic Girl in the 1940's.

Bugsy Siegel's arrival in Los Angeles marked the beginning of the end for organized crime in the City of Angeles. LOS ANGELES TIMES PHOTO

When Howard Hughes was arrested for Vehicular Homidie it was Archie MacDonald who convinced the lone witness to charge his story at the coroner's inquest. LOS ANGELES TIMES PHOTO

By the mid-1930's, Gaynell had obtained her financial fortune. She was living the good life. Sadly, Gaynell soon discovered money could not buy happiness.

Florence Clark (adult) spent a great deal of time with her "two daughters" Betty Ann (older girl) and Marion (in Betty Ann's arms). The two girls were like sisters from an early age.

Renny Rockwell at the Pottenger Sanitarium. Two months after this picture was taken, Renny passed away. He was thirty years old.

Bob and Betty Ann – Early 1947.

Seventeen-year old Betty Ann Rockwell.

1942: Bob MacDonald shortly after his commission in the U.S. Army.

Gaynell was 17, Renny 19 when they married in 1919.

Seventeen-year-old Marion Clark.

Robert Hull – A dashing military man.

Gaynell worked side by side with Los Angeles Mayor Franklin Shaw (middle) and Los Angeles Police Chief James Davis (right), two of the most powerful and corrupt men in Los Angeles History. The other person is Rafael Heredia, LA Mexican Consul.

Benjamin "Bugsy" Siegel and his friend, actor George Raft.

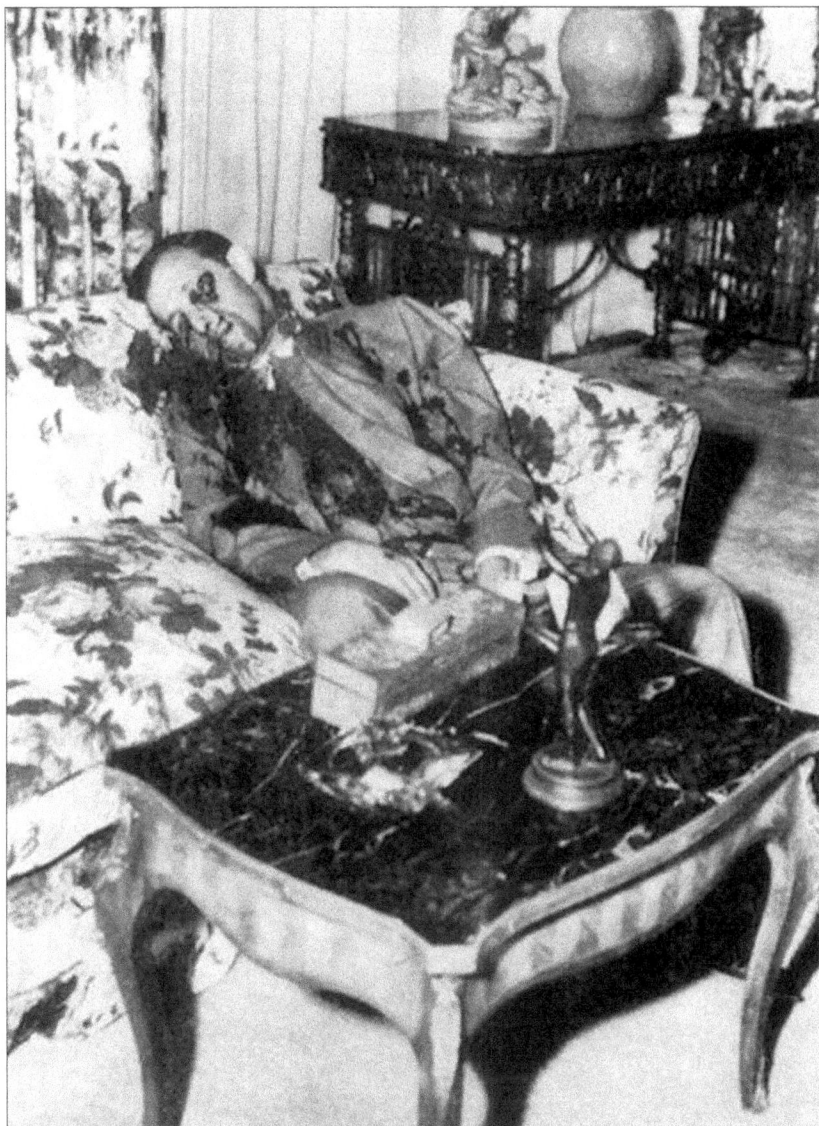

The late Benjamin "Bugsy" Siegel.

Police inspect the location where Benjamin Siegel's killer committed the hit.
HERALD EXAMINER PHOTO

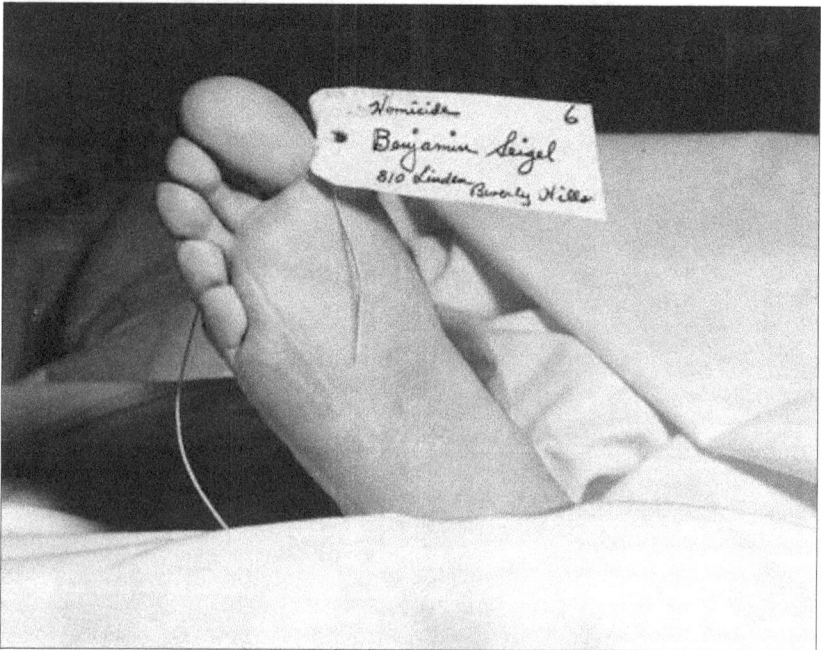

Siegel's toe tag in the morgue.

Jack Dragna. HERALD EXAMINER PHOTO

"Bugsy" Siegel's legacy: The Flamingo Hotel in Las Vegas. UNLV University Libraries

Chapter Fourteen
Wedding Bell Blues

"I first met Archie MacDonald in the mid-'30s," Gaynell recalled. "As general manager of the Hughes Tool Company, Archie was in and out of City Hall all the time. In all my dealings with him, I found Archie to be very nice and very professional. He was simply a good man."

After her marriage to Ralph Applegate, Gaynell began attending many of the same social functions as Archie. It was at one of those events that Gaynell discovered MacDonald had a son who just happened to be an eligible bachelor.

"I knew Betty Ann was going to marry Bob the first time I saw him," Gaynell said. "Bob was handsome and came from one of the wealthiest families in Southern California. In my eyes, Bob had the potential to be a very suitable son-in-law."

"Without a doubt, Betty Ann was attracted to Bob," Marion recalled. "When he wanted to be, Bob was a thoroughly charming man."

After a few months of dating, Betty Ann decided to take her budding relationship with Bob to the next level. It was an event that had enormous consequences.

"Bob took Betty Ann to Catalina Island on Howard Hughes' boat," Marion said. "They spent the day having fun in the sun and the night dancing at the Grand Ballroom to the music of one of the big bands. On the trip home, there were a romantic moon and a bottle of wine. One thing led to another and the next thing she knew Betty Ann was doing the unspeakable. She had premarital scx with Bob MacDonald.

"By the next day, Betty Ann realized she had made an enormous mistake in sleeping with Bob. She told him they needed to cool things down a bit. Betty Ann came to realize her courtship with Bob was a major error.

There was a rumor floating about that Betty Ann was in a relationship with another man besides Bob, but like most rumors, without proof there was nothing that could be substantiated.

One thing was certain, after she had stepped away from Bob, Betty Ann decided to end the relationship. A few weeks after that decision however, Betty Ann discovered she was pregnant and at that point, everything changed. In the 1940s, if you were a seventeen-year-old girl with child, the nineteen-year-old father of your baby was a staunch Catholic—or more importantly, his parents were, which was precisely what Mr. MacDonald and Mrs. MacDonald were, you got married. That's what Betty Ann and Bob did.

"Initially, there were plans for a huge wedding. Gaynell had expectations that the affair was going to be a gala celebration. However, when Betty Ann started to show early, the very public wedding was changed to a more subdued private affair, and on June 2, 1941, Bob, and Betty Ann were married.

"When Bob married Betty Ann, he was not ready to grow up and accept the responsibility of adulthood, let alone marriage," Gaynell once recalled. "He was a young man who had just acquired a taste for wine, women, song, dance, and gambling. Bob believed he had done the right thing by marrying Betty Ann, but he also thought being married shouldn't interfere with the fun in his life. It didn't."

* * * * *

The first few months of the MacDonald marriage went along fairly smoothly. Shortly after the baby was born in the fall of 1941, however, the matrimonial bliss began to unravel rather quickly.

Prior to the shotgun affair, Betty Ann was aware of Bob's taste for a few vices. She knew he liked to drink, smoke, and gamble, but she did not realize the extent of how serious her husband's addiction to gambling was until after she and Bob had exchanged their marriage vows.

"No doubt about it," Nick Moretta once said. "The boy liked to gamble. The first time I saw Bob gamble, it was out on the 'Rex,' one of the gambling boats Jack Dragna ran off the coast. It was before Bob, and Betty Ann were married, so I bet he was only about seventeen. I watched him drop about three thousand bucks in about three hours. Three thousand dollars was a lot of money in the early '40s. Hell, three thousand dollars is a lot of money, period."

Initially, Bob's gambling junkets were somewhat sporadic. As time passed, however, his evening escapades became more and more frequent, and Betty Ann was left alone more often than not. When Betty Ann expressed her concerns to her husband about his regular late nights out and the constant smell of alcohol on his breath, Bob countered by claiming Betty Ann was nagging and not giving him the room he needed to be a happy man.

"Betty Ann was disturbed by Bob's behavior shortly after they were married," Marion said. "I was the only one she could talk with about things. Gaynell never wanted to hear it. Bob's link to the Hughes Empire assured him 'Prince Charming' status with his mother-in-law. In Gaynell's eyes, Bob could do no wrong.

"Betty Ann was not a woman who whined or complained about too many things in life. So, when she expressed her misgivings about Bob, I listened.

"There was one incident that particularly bothered Betty Ann. Shortly before their marriage, Bob went away for the weekend with a group of friends. On the way home, he was in an automobile accident. Two occupants in the other vehicle were killed, and the young man riding with Bob, the son of movie star Faye Bainter, was severely injured. Bob had been drinking, and the accident was clearly his fault.

"At the very least, Bob should have been charged with vehicular manslaughter for the accident. Archie, however, pursued an out-of-court arrangement with the parties involved. The case never made it into court and Bob was never penalized.

"I think, more than anything, Bob's lack of remorse concerning that accident troubled Betty Ann," Marion said. "She couldn't understand why being responsible for the death of two people didn't have more of an impact on her husband."

Having a cold-hearted husband would become the least of Betty Ann's concerns. Bob's drinking, gambling, and infidelities began to appear shortly after the start of World War II, thereby creating more heartache and pain than most seventeen-year-old girls should ever have to endure in their lives.

Chapter Fifteen
The War Years

Shortly after the start of World War II, Gaynell and Nick were married in Reno, Nevada.

In 1942, Marion Clark met Robert Hull. Hull, an army man, was stationed in Los Angeles, California. Marion, just seventeen, was still in high school. The two met in a soda shop in Hawthorne, California, in March.

"Robert was a very dashing twenty-four-year-old," Marion recalled. "He was exceptionally good-looking in uniform."

Robert was quick to gain the approval of the Clark and Applegate families, with the exception of the lone hold-out, Gaynell. While Gaynell believed Robert was a good man, she also knew that if Hull made the military his career, he would never be a very rich one.

"Gaynell was very motherly toward me," Marion said. "She sat me in the kitchen and told me it was just as easy to marry a rich man as it was to marry a poor one. I knew what she was saying, but in June of 1942, when Robert proposed, I accepted. I wanted to be happy, not rich.

"After I made my decision to marry Robert, Gaynell was nothing but supportive. She took him in and never again expressed concern or disappointment with my selection of a spouse."

On November 2, 1942, Robert James Hull and Marion Florence Clark ran off to downtown Los Angeles, where they became husband and wife in a brief ceremony at City Hall.

"Gaynell and Betty Ann had a get-together for Robert and me. Gaynell offered a very nice toast. She wished us all the happiness in the world and hoped that our children would be healthy. She then giggled and stated she had one request. Her request was that, for the sake of God and the sanity of the family, if we had a male child first, not to name the baby Robert, Jr. Having a son named Robert Rockwell, a son-in-law named Robert MacDonald, and now, with her niece marrying Robert Hull, another Robert in the family would just be too damn confusing."

* * * * *

Christmas 1942

Robert Hull was stationed at the Headquarters Battery of the 205th Coast Artillery. The base was located at the Veterans' Home, at the corner of Sawtelle and Wilshire in Los Angeles. That location was just minutes away from the residence of Nick and Gaynell Moretta, who lived on Hudson Drive, a few blocks off Wilshire.

"During the early part of the war," Robert Hull said, "I probably had dinner with Gaynell and Nick two or three times a week. It wasn't uncommon for Nick and Gaynell to have friends over on the nights I stopped by. It was through Nick that I met Jack Dragna. My first contact with Dragna came in 1942, just before Christmas. Nick and Gaynell had asked me to stop by and pick up some Christmas gifts they had for Marion and me.

"When I got to the Moretta house, Nick and some of his friends were playing cards. Gaynell insisted I stay for dinner; then Nick insisted I sit in for a few hands of cards. I was introduced to Jack Dragna, his brother Tom, and another man named Momo.

"While playing cards, I remember Jack Dragna asked me a number of questions regarding my military service, the way the war was going, how I liked being in the service, and how much I was making. I told Jack I made fifty-eight dollars a month. After Dragna stopped laughing, everyone started speaking Italian.

"Shortly after, I found myself in a big pot hand—about three hundred dollars. I was going to fold several times but kept getting coaxed into upping my bet by Nick and Jack's friends.

"Finally, Dragna called the hand. I laid down two pairs. I knew I didn't have a great hand, but I missed my full house, so I decided to try to bluff my way to the win. Dragna studied me for a minute, then shook his head in concession and threw his hand face-down on the table.

"'Fuck,' Dragna said. 'Beats what I got.'

"Dragna pushed the pot toward me with a smile," Robert continued. "Then Jack and the other men called it a night, pushed away from the table, wished Gaynell, Nick, and me, a merry Christmas, and then left the residence.

"I helped Nick clean up. When I went back to the table, I noticed Dragna's cards were still in the same position as when he left. I had to see what he had. I flipped his cards over and discovered he had folded while holding a full house. We had a good Christmas that year, and it was due, in part, to Jack Dragna."

Robert was invited for dinner on several occasions, and whenever Jack Dragna was at the Moretta home, he always made it a point to be very cordial to the younger man. "More than anything, Dragna seemed appreciative of the fact that I was serving our country," Hull said.

By no means did Robert Hull and Jack Dragna have any type of relationship other than informal and in passing. When the two men did have conversations, the topic always revolved around the war and how Hull's military life was going. Hull would see Dragna approximately a half-dozen times in his life, each time at the Moretta home. Robert Hull's interaction with one of the most ruthless crime bosses in Southern California was a positive one.

"Jack Dragna and the people around him were always straight up with me," Robert said. "In my book, Jack Dragna was a pretty good Joe."

Positive memories were not exclusive to Robert Hull, but to Marion as well. When Robert Hull's unit was shipped out for a six-month assignment in Texas, Marion Hull thought she would not be provided the chance to see her husband before he left the states for Europe. A before Robert's transfer overseas, Marion discovered she could have a seventy-two-hour visit with her husband if she could find transportation to Texas.

"Travel during the war was tough to achieve, especially for dependent wives," Marion said. "For thirteen days in a row, I arrived at Union Station at 6:00 a.m., placed my name on the space-available list, and then waited to be assigned a seat on the train. For thirteen straight days, my travel request was denied, and for thirteen days straight, I returned home only to get up the next day and try again.

"Betty Ann called my mother to see why I hadn't called her from Texas," Marion said. "When Mom told her I was still in Los Angeles because I kept getting bumped, Betty Ann told Mom she was going to make a call to Jack and that she would pick me up the next morning and take me to the train station herself.

"The next morning, Betty Ann came to Mom's house, picked me up, and drove me to Union Station. We got there ten minutes before the train was scheduled to depart. Betty Ann went to the front of the train, stepped aboard, and then a few moments later, returned to me with a porter. He took my luggage and loaded it aboard the train. Betty Ann gave me a hug and a kiss and told me to have a great trip. I just looked at her dumbfounded. Betty Ann chuckled. 'Call me when you get there,' she said, as she walked away.

"The next three days, I spent a luxurious ride in a private room with first-class service, got to visit with Robert for three days, then came back to California the same way I went to Texas—first class.

"Clearly, Betty Ann, with a little help from Jack Dragna, had made the arrangements necessary to accomplish the feat of getting me from point A to point B and back to point A. It was wonderful for them to do that for me; otherwise, I wouldn't have seen Robert for a long while."

* * * * *

March 1942

"During the early part of the war, I found out Bob MacDonald was into Jack for a little over fifty-thousand dollars" Nick Moretta once said. "I also found out it was the second time Bob had run up such a huge debt; the first time was before Betty Ann and Bob got married, and that time Bob had lost about 35,000. Bob made good on it, so Jack let him extend to fifty grand.

"After the war began, Jack wanted to get all outstanding debts cleared," Nick continued. "There were a number of guys who lost big money, got shipped out, and left Jack holding the bag. When Jack made a call for markers to be cleared, Bob got a bit of an attitude. Well, Jack Dragna wasn't about to take shit from some twenty-year-old punk kid, so he sent a couple of fellas to pay Bob a visit. The guys found Bob and beat the shit outta him pretty good. That day, Bob went home and cleared out his bank accounts and gave Jack about half of what he owed him.

"After Betty Ann discovered most of the money from their bank account gone, she confronted Bob," Nick continued. "Bob became argumentative with her over things; then he became violent. That was the first time Bob ever struck her. It was something that didn't sit well with a lot of people, Jack Dragna included."

"Betty Ann couldn't believe Bob had hit her," Marion said. "She packed her bags and went to Gaynell's. The next day, she went to a lawyer, and then to the church to explore the possibility of obtaining an annulment. It was an ugly time."

In the meantime, Bob went to his father for help. That wasn't the first time he'd asked him to help bail him out of his gambling debts. When Bob went to his father this second time, however, Archie said no to Bob's request for approximately $25,000.

"Bob was in a panic," Nick recalled. "Even with the bank accounts drained, he was short the money he owed Jack. To complicate things, he had beaten his wife. She had left him, and everyone in the family wanted a piece of his ass because he had gotten physical with her."

Shortly after that event, Robert MacDonald accepted a commission in the United States Army and then volunteered for service overseas. As a newlywed, the father of a newborn child, and the godson of Howard Hughes, Bob MacDonald could have easily obtained an exemption from serving in the military.

"The fact that Bob volunteered for the army shocked a lot of people," Marion said. "No one but family knew Bob's heroic call to duty was just an attempt to run from the demons in his life."

* * * * *

August 1943

Gaynell decided the women of the family needed a retreat. A trip to Bridgeport was perfect. The cabin, which was originally purchased by Ralph Applegate in the late 1920s, had become a place of escape for Gaynell.

"Going to Bridgeport and experiencing the beauty of the secluded mountain town always seemed to raise everyone's spirits," Marion said. "Bridgeport was the source of many pleasant memories for all of us. Gaynell knew going to the cabin was the best remedy for the wartime blues, so we tried to go as often as we could. There was one particular trip, however, where we encountered a very non-relaxing situation.

"After spending several hours on the road, we finally reached downtown Bridgeport, and three miles later, we pulled into the drive at the cabin. As soon as the car came to a stop, several men carrying weapons surrounded the car.

"Nick came running from the cabin, screaming, 'No, no, no,' as he ran toward the car. 'It's okay; it's okay.' As it turned out, the men with guns were members of Jack's 'family,' and they were in hiding at the cabin. The Dragnas had used the cabin on several occasions, but when they did, they usually cleared it with Nick, who in turn cleared it with Gaynell."

"This particular trip, Nick made no mention of Jack or the boys going to Bridgeport," Gaynell said. "Nick had left for Reno a few days earlier and was going to meet us at the cabin. That's all I knew. So when these men came running at us with guns in hand, it pissed me off."

"After several minutes of screaming at Nick, Gaynell returned to the car and informed us that our plans had just changed," Marion said. "Our retreat to the cabin had just become a retreat to Reno, compliments of Jack and Nick.

"Gaynell left the cabin with tires spinning and gravel flying. For the next thirty minutes, she drove the car like a bat out of Hell back to town and pulled into the country store. She exited the car, slammed the door shut, and went into the store without saying a word to any of us.

"A few minutes later, she returned with several cold sodas in hand. After giving each one of us one and taking a long drink from her own, she started giggling like a school girl. 'Did anyone else almost shit their pants when they saw those guns?' she said. We all started laughing hysterically, then we went on to Reno and had a wonderful three-day holiday."

* * * * *

During World War II, most married women were not very happy people, especially if their husbands were serving in the military overseas. Betty Ann MacDonald, however, seemed to be the exception to that rule.

"At first, I thought it was strange that Betty Ann was so giddy," Marion said. "Some of her friends were telling me she was on cloud nine because she was having an affair. I thought, *No, that couldn't be.* Then I thought, *Well, Hell's bells, why not?*

"There was gossip that Betty Ann and Howard Hughes had become intimate friends. Hughes had a tremendous reputation for being a ladies' man, so I think it was natural to assume the two were having an affair, especially since they seemed to be becoming closer and closer friends. Hughes had taken quite a liking to Betty Ann during the war."

"Howard liked Betty Ann's no-bullshit attitude and appreciated the fact she wasn't in awe of him," Archie MacDonald once said. "She was one of the few people at social events who didn't feel the need to kiss Howard's ass, and Howard liked that."

"As the war started to wind down, however, Betty Ann had to make a choice. For the first time in her adult life, she was happy and in love. With Bob coming home, Betty Ann found herself in a heart-wrenching situation. She had found a man she could make a life with; however, her husband would soon be returning from the war. I wasn't sure what she was going to do, and then I found out from Gaynell that Betty Ann had sent Bob a 'Dear John' letter. She had decided to be happy. Ironically, it was Betty Ann's letter that caused Bob to do what he did in Aachen.

* * * * *

"Hitting Betty Ann pissed off everybody," Nick once said. "Archie, Howard, Jack, Gaynell, all of us were so angry. Jack was especially pissed. He wanted to kill Bob then and there."

Gaynell and Renny Rockwell, back in the late '20s, had asked Dragna to become Betty Ann's godfather. He was honored to do so, and he grew to like the girl; thought she was "spunky."

Nick Moretta: "Jack felt it was his responsibility to take care of Betty Ann, even if it meant having Bob taken care of. I think Bob's fear of what Jack was going to do to him for beating up his goddaughter was the primary factor in his running off and joining the army. What was crazy about Bob joining up was, if Jack had wanted to kill him for not paying his debt or for whacking Betty Ann around, he could have made it happen no matter where that little cocksucker ran to.

"When Betty Ann was considering leaving Bob, toward the end of the war, I think Jack put a hit out on Bob. The hit never happened, and later on, Jack found out that the shooter ended up getting killed in action. If the shooter hadn't been killed, my guess is Bob would have never made it back from Europe, let alone made it back as a hero. The little shit was a hero—sure he was!"

* * * * *

As the winner of two Purple Hearts, a Bronze Star, and a Silver Star, if one didn't know the story behind the story, Bob MacDonald's military career appeared to contain an act of tremendous heroism. The official military record stated that, during a battle in the town of Aachen, German troops caught Bob MacDonald's unit in an ambush. The men scrambled for cover, and several soldiers, including Bob, found safety in an abandoned beerhouse. While the men managed to get under cover, they also realized that, unless they did something, it would only be a matter of time before the German troops identified their position and brought in reinforcements.

As the story goes, MacDonald grabbed his rifle, rested the barrel of the weapon on a window ledge, and began picking off German soldiers one by one. No one in his outfit knew of Bob's abilities with a rifle, but no doubt they were all pleased to discover that he was an expert marksman.

After running out of ammunition, Bob strapped a satchel of grenades across his chest and made his way to the farthest point of the city. Once out of harm's way, he found a bicycle with no tires, only rims, and rode down the cobblestone street, killing German troops along the way, thereby facilitating the escape of his company. Great story had it ended there.

"Bob was decorated for bravery for what he did that day in Aachen," Betty Ann once said. "Later, he confessed to me that his deed was a suicide attempt gone awry."

"The truth of the matter was Bob was going to kill himself," Robert Hull stated, in confirmation of Betty Ann's statement. "Bob told me he had gotten Betty Ann's letter just before the battle of Aachen. With the news that his wife was leaving him, and with a massive debt looming over his head upon his return, he thought the coward's way out was going to be his easiest escape from life.

"Bob did everything in the official accounting they say he did. When you leave out the fact that he was trying to kill himself when he strapped the grenades around his body and attacked the Germans, it sounds pretty heroic."

While Bob's act did save the lives of many men, the fact that he was singing "Boogie Woogie Bugle Boy of Company B" as he was throwing his grenades suggests something amiss with this heroic deed.

"Bob had received Betty Ann's 'Dear John' letter the day before the incident at Aachen," Gaynell once said. "He then wrote a letter to Betty Ann and told her that, because things with his father were strained, because he still owed a lot of money to gangsters, because his wife was leaving him, and because his life was so screwed up, he was going to go out in a blaze of glory."

Betty Ann got the letter a few days after she was notified by army personnel of Bob's hospitalization for the injuries he suffered during a heroic deed in Aachen.

"There's a scene in the movie *Dances with Wolves* that fits Bob MacDonald's situation in Germany perfectly," Marion Hull once said. "Kevin Costner's character decides to kill himself by riding on his horse in front of the enemy. In the end, they can't kill him, and he becomes somewhat of a hero. Bob's bike trip down the cobblestone street in Aachen was the same damn thing."

Ironically, MacDonald's suicide attempt was embraced as an act of heroism, and the perception of his deed gave his family, especially Archie, a renewed sense of optimism that his son would become a productive, mature adult.

Gaynell: "I always sensed Archie knew Bob's heroic deed wasn't what it appeared to be, but how can you fault Archie for wanting it to be as it appeared? Bob was his child—a lost child, but nonetheless, if the story had been true, there was hope for Bob. What parent wouldn't want that for one of their children?"

* * * * *

"Betty Ann spent the last few months of the war in complete torment," Marion Hull said. "She was in love, and she knew her 'Captain' was her only chance at true happiness."

As Bob's return from Europe drew nearer and nearer, Betty Ann had to make a decision—stay in her marriage or end it. If she left Bob, she and her child would be cast out from the family. She would be happy, but her son would be completely alienated and cut off from his blood relatives.

Betty Ann ended her affair. While disappointed, Betty Ann's captain accepted his love's decision with grace, dignity, and great sadness.

"It was the first, and only, time in her life Betty Ann had known true love," Marion said.

Gaynell never criticized Betty Ann's affair, and in many ways, understood her daughter's plight. She had married Renny Rockwell out of necessity, much like Betty Ann had married Bob. Gaynell then found her happiness with another man, Nick Moretta. While very sympathetic to Betty Ann's situation, she admittedly breathed a sigh of relief when her daughter decided to stay with Bob MacDonald.

The identity of Betty's army captain will forever remain anonymous. Betty Ann and her soul mate were star-crossed lovers who were brought together by the tragic circumstances of war, then sorrowfully separated when the global conflict ended.

Bob MacDonald returned from the European theater to a grand welcome-home party. While his heroic act, which saved a handful of men, was acknowledged by Archie, in the very next breath the elder MacDonald also thanked Howard Hughes for saving an entire nation.

Chapter Sixteen
Homecoming Blues

"In the months following Bob's return from Europe, there was hope for change," Gaynell once said. "Archie had given Bob the money to clear his debt with Jack Dragna, and Bob's sins were forgiven. We all hoped better times were on the way. In the end, however, nothing was different. Bob was Bob; all he seemed to want to do was drink, gamble, and chase women."

"Everyone was trying to help Bob," Marion said. "Archie, Howard, and even Gaynell were trying to find Bob a trade that he liked. Gaynell even offered Bob a job. When the war started, on the advice of Howard Hughes and Archie, Gaynell had purchased a galvanizing plant in Vernon.

"At the time, Advanced Galvanizing was the only galvanizing plant in the Los Angeles area, so Gaynell was making a small fortune. Bob Rockwell, Gaynell's son, was running the plant back then, and he was more than willing to take his brother-in-law under his wing, but Bob MacDonald didn't want any part of working."

"The galvanizing business was fairly easy," Gaynell once said. "We used an assembly line process to clean and prepare a piece of metal for dipping into a vat of molten zinc. That process gave a protective coating to the metal and assisted in the prevention of corrosion. I offered Bob a job in quality control, but he simply didn't want any part of it."

Instead, Bob MacDonald simply gambled his days away. Betty Ann had decided she was going to focus on being a mother. She had a five-year-old son and, as a result of her renewed commitment to her husband and her marriage, another child on the way.

"Betty Ann was miserable with Bob," Marion said. "Any time she even talked of ending her marriage with Bob, however, Gaynell had a fit. She fought Betty Ann every time divorce was mentioned."

Gaynell had a good thing going. Archie was giving her financial advice, and being tied to a family with links to Howard Hughes was giving her the prestige she craved. She had it all: wealth, power, and social status. Betty Ann, however, was living in a loveless marriage."

In the spring of 1946, Betty Ann gave birth to her second child, and for a brief period of time, there was happiness in the MacDonald household. With the birth of his daughter, Bob calmed down a bit, leaving Betty Ann with a ray of hope that her spouse would become a loving father and husband. Once again, her hopes went unrealized.

Life was different for many after World War II. So much had changed in the world. For the Rockwell family, however, the time had come to get back the good old days.

"During the Fourth of July holiday, we decided to reinstate the family tradition of barbecuing on the beach," Marion said. "It was the first time since the war started that the entire family had been able to come together.

"It was just like old times—the spread was awesome, the weather was perfect. Only one thing could have made it better: Betty Ann and Gaynell could have been there.

"We didn't expect either Betty Ann or Gaynell at the barbecue. Betty Ann had just given birth, and Gaynell had been invited to attend a party in Newport Beach, which was being put on by Howard Hughes. It was a big party for Hughes, since a few days later he was going to make a test flight of a new airplane. We joked about Gaynell actually choosing to attend the catered Hughes event when she could have had the barbequed pork, potato salad, and roasted corn that we were having.

"The sun had just set, and the men had the bonfire raging. I saw a figure appear from the darkness, and as the person came closer, I realized it was Betty Ann with her children in tow. We were all so happy to see her and the kids. It was a very nice surprise.

"A while later, we were even more shocked when Nick showed up. Nick was never comfortable at big events and did not share Gaynell's love for being in the limelight. Instead, he chose to stop by a street-side fruit vendor and bring several mangos for the pork."

"Nick loved to have barbequed pork sandwiches with mango," Robert Hull added. "I thought *Good God that has to be horrible.* Then I tried it and found out Nick was onto something. It was good!

"After Betty Ann and Nick showed up, Gaynell arrived a short while later with Howard Hughes. It was the damnedest thing. Here was the wealthiest man in the world coming to the Rockwell family barbeque. I had heard how bizarre he was becoming and how aloof he was, but you know something, he was just as normal as normal could be.

"Betty Ann had a great relationship with Howard. That evening, Hughes sat by the fire and chatted with her for about an hour, and then he spent the rest of his time around the bonfire with the rest of the family. It was as if he had known us for much of his life. It was a strange night, to say the least, but we all had a great time."

Tragically, on July 7, 1946, just three days after the Rockwell barbecue, Howard Hughes was critically injured when the XF-11 plane he was flying lost power over Beverly Hills. The accident happened less than a mile from the MacDonald home, and when Betty Ann heard the news of the accident, she hurried to the crash site on foot.

By the time she arrived at the scene at 808 North Whittier, Hughes had already been transported to the hospital. When Betty Ann looked about the rubble and saw what was left of the plane, she was sure Howard was dead. She suddenly collapsed in the street and began to sob.

"A number of people had come to the accident scene to be looky-loos," Gaynell stated. "When they saw Betty Ann bawling in the street, not one of them knew who she was or how special Howard Hughes was to her. In a way, she was Howard Hughes' best kept secret."

"The next day, Archie and Bob went to the crash site," Gaynell recalled. "While the military had secured the area, Archie, as a significant associate of Hughes, was granted access to the scene of the accident."

"Howard's plane had lost power, so he was trying to ditch the craft on one of the fairways at the Beverly Hills Country Club," Archie once said. "He came up a few hundred yards short and hit the roof of a house on North Linden, before crashing between two houses on North Whittier."

Ironically, the Hughes aircraft struck a home at 805 North Linden, just a few hundred feet from what would be the scene of Bugsy Siegel's grizzly murder a year later.

"It was a horrible day for the MacDonald family," Marion recalled. "No one knew if Howard was going to live or die."

Over the course of a few weeks, Howard's health improved, and the MacDonald family was able to breathe a sigh of relief. Hughes had proved all the doctors wrong by surviving the accident.

"From July of 1946 through early March of 1947, life was fairly uneventful," Marion said. "Bob had become discreet about how much money he was losing and also discreet with his affairs. Then, in March of 1947, all Hell broke loose."

One afternoon, Betty Ann had returned home from an outing to find both her husband and a redhead naked in the backyard. Bob had been cheating on Betty Ann ever since their marriage began. While this was not the first occasion, she'd witnessed her husband having sex with another woman.

After shooing his guest away, Bob became furious with his wife. Upset with the fact that she had allowed their son to witness his indiscretion, he exploded in a fit of rage.

"He gave Betty Ann a horrible beating that day," Marion recalled. "She refused to go to the doctor and had to wear a pair of oversized sunglasses for a few weeks to cover up the bruises. Wife abuse wasn't talked about in the '40s. It was ignored. The thinking was that if no one talked about horrible things, they might not have happened. Well, they did happen.

"Betty Ann wanted out of her marriage," Marion continued. "She'd had enough. Bob had delivered the straw that had broken the camel's back. Betty Ann packed up her things, the children, her belongings, and left the house.

"It would have been easy for Betty Ann to leave Bob. She was financially independent, so, unlike many women of the time, she didn't have to rely on a husband for monetary support.

"When Betty Ann stated she was leaving Bob, Nick was the only one who supported her. Gaynell steadfastly opposed the break-up. Archie convinced Betty Ann to let him get Bob into counseling and seek help for his problems. He wanted her to agree to stay in the marriage, and let him try to save his son."

Out of respect, Betty Ann honored Archie's request and remained in her marriage to Robert Crosbie MacDonald. She was going to give him one more chance.

After Betty Ann decided to stay with Bob, Nick Moretta expressed his reservations about the reconciliation. "Nick was not a very dominating man," Marion said. "I only saw Nick stand up to Gaynell one time in his life. It concerned Betty Ann and Bob's marriage, and it was a dandy.

"Mom and I were having dinner with Gaynell and Nick shortly after Betty Ann had agreed to give Bob one more chance with their marriage. Gaynell was boasting about how she was the facilitator in getting the two back together and how wonderful Bob and Betty Ann's lives were going to be. Nick was eating his meal in complete silence, which was a very uncommon thing for Nick to do, while Gaynell just kept going on and on about how wonderful it was that Bob was changing his ways. She was so happy Betty Ann and Bob had agreed to work things out. Finally, Nick pushed away from the table and began yelling at Gaynell in Italian.

"'You're wrong on this, Gay,' Nick then said in English.

"'Don't tell me my business,' Gaynell snapped.

"'Somebody needs to tell you your business, 'cuz with this here, your head's all fucked up. You're not thinking right.'

"With that, Nick muttered something else in Italian, excused himself to Robert and me, then stormed out of the house. Gaynell didn't know what to do. She merely sat at the table like a deer caught in headlights. Nick's reaction had taken her totally by surprise, and more than likely, hit too close to home."

Nick Moretta knew about degenerate gamblers. He knew Bob was an alcohol abuser and a womanizer. Nothing in Nick's book, not even the tie to Hughes, was worth Betty Ann living a life of misery. Nick was scared for Betty Ann, scared for her future, and scared Gaynell's counsel may have put Betty Ann into harm's way.

Chapter Seventeen
Bugsy

Benjamin "Bugsy" Siegel was born on February 28, 1905. Siegel's parents had emigrated from Russia several years earlier, to the Williamsburg section of Brooklyn, New York. The neighborhood Bugsy grew up in consisted of people from Jewish, Irish, and Italian descent.

In his youth, Siegel formed several friendships, the most significant of which was with another young Jewish boy by the name of Meyer Lansky. It didn't take too long before Lansky and Siegel formed a gang known as the "Bugs and Meyer Mob." The two boys ran street gambling games, developed a protection racket, committed burglaries, and eventually entered into a murder-for-hire business.

Charlie "Lucky" Lucania (later changed to Luciano) met both Benjamin Siegel and Meyer Lansky on the streets of New York. Luciano enjoyed strong-arming pennies from the kids on the street. When Lucky offered Lansky his protection for Meyer's pocket change, and Meyer refused, he instantly won Luciano's respect. Then, after Luciano discovered Lansky's friend, Benjamin Siegel, was just as bold and brash as Lansky, an instant friendship was born.

By 1919, Joe "the Boss" Masseria, considered the kingpin of the New York Mafia and one of the most feared mobsters in New York, wanted to flex his muscle in Brooklyn, but couldn't due to the influence of Siegel, Lansky, and Charlie "Lucky" Luciano. He decided to cut the up-and-coming gangsters in on a piece of his action. The piece the gang was given was small, but this opportunity got their feet in the door with one of the most powerful men in the world of organized crime.

While Luciano aligned with Masseria, Siegel, and Lansky decided to combine forces with Arnold Rothstein, the mastermind behind the fixing of the 1919 World Series. Rothstein was convinced gambling could be promoted as a recreational activity and was seeking young, aggressive underlings to help him promote this philosophy. Rothstein also believed that, if gamblers were provided with good-looking accommodations in which to lose their money, most would. As it turned out, Rothstein's beliefs had a profound impact on Siegel, who later designed and developed the Flamingo Hotel in Las Vegas, Nevada.

Siegel and Lansky's relationship with Rothstein ended abruptly after Rothstein was murdered over a card game. After the death of their boss, they joined forces with Luciano. Once they combined their strengths, the group decided to take over the rackets, not just in New York, but nationally. Joe Masseria and Sal Maranzana were assassinated in 1931, leaving Luciano, Lansky, and Siegel in control of their own Mob family.

In the mid-1930s, a decision was made to dispatch Ben Siegel to California. Siegel's mission in coming to Los Angeles was to bring Southern California up to speed in terms of gambling operations and make the Mob a coast-to-coast operation.

Jack Dragna was the main man in regards to organized crime in Los Angeles. Siegel's arrival in Southern California concerned Dragna for several reasons. First and foremost was the fact that Jack Dragna knew Siegel's brash personality would clash with L.A.'s philosophy on vice in the City of Angels. Dragna did not demand complete control over game-room operations, did not believe in being high profile, and did not believe in solving business matters with guns publicly blazing. Ben Siegel was just the opposite.

Siegel believed gambling operations on the West Coast could be run the same way as gambling operations on the East Coast. Siegel did not understand that the people who lived in California were different from the people who lived in New York. Siegel's biggest blunder was that he didn't understand the good people of New York City and the fine citizens of Los Angeles had different tolerances for vice, as well.

Dragna had cultivated an organization that was dependent upon a delicate balance of power between the crooks, the politicians, the police, and the citizenry of Los Angeles. With everyone getting a piece of the pie, everyone stayed happy, and to some extent, tolerant of any non-violent vice.

When Siegel arrived in Los Angeles in the mid-1930s, Franklin Shaw was in his heyday as mayor. Prostitution, gambling, and bootlegging liquor were in full swing. The profits were modest according to Mob standards, but they were steady. Siegel wanted that to change.

At the time, there were two wire services: the Continental and the Trans American. Those two services provided bookies across the nation with any and all information on horse races coming from California. California bookies predominately used Continental, the service provided by James Ragan, an independent operator from Chicago. That did not sit well with Siegel's group since Trans America was in a partnership with Al Capone, who was more than generous with the revenues of that wire service to Luciano, Lansky, and Siegel.

Despite six years of strong-arming efforts to remove Ragan, Siegel's ability to oust Continental had proved unsuccessful, so he resorted to what he knew best, which was murder. Once Siegel's goons gunned down Ragan, Continental's service evaporated, allowing Trans America to become the lone source of gambling information on the West Coast and the most lucrative business that the Meyer and Bugs gang had.

Siegel next expanded his gambling base by getting involved in horse racing at Santa Anita and boxing at the Olympic Auditorium in downtown Los Angeles. After securing those two venues, he turned his attention to the motion picture industry and gained control over the Hollywood Extras Union. All three ventures netted the gangster a sizable income.

Siegel then tried to unite gaming operators in Southern California under the umbrella of the East Coast syndicate. That didn't sit well with too many people, especially those who were going to have to share their profits with the boys from New York.

Many of the gambling czars grumbled at Siegel's idea, but only Les Bruneman, an old-time Los Angeles gambling boss, openly spoke out against Siegel's plan to unite. On October 28, 1937, in an attempt to show his muscle, Siegel had Les Bruneman murdered.

Bruneman's murder was nothing short of a public execution. Siegel had violated the first rule of crime in Los Angeles. The killing of Bruneman was the straw that broke the camel's back for the usually indifferent citizens of Southern California and they began to re-examine their tolerance for vice. With one murder, Benjamin "Bugsy" Siegel had destroyed the stability of a corruption machine that had been in place in the City of Angels since the early 1920s.

Within months of the Bruneman murder, the house of cards built by Jack Dragna and Franklin Shaw began to fall apart. Shaw was recalled from office in 1938, and the purging of the police department soon followed, leaving Jack Dragna without many of his strongest allies.

By the early 1940s, Siegel's crime efforts in Los Angeles were becoming more and more constrained. During World War II, Siegel managed to make money for himself and his partners back east, but Bugsy's shtick in Los Angeles was growing old, and his profits were dwindling.

Eventually, Luciano, Lansky, Siegel and their associates planted their flags in Las Vegas, Nevada and obtained a controlling interest in the El Rancho Hotel and Casino.

By the end of the war, the group had discovered a half-built hotel in the Mojave Desert. The "Flamingo Hotel and Casino" was the brainchild of Billy Wilkerson, the publisher of the Hollywood Reporter. Wilkerson had run into financial difficulties after he squandered hundreds of thousands of the construction funds on gambling, it left the door open for Luciano and his associates to move in and "help" Wilkerson complete the Flamingo.

Of course the mob would need someone to oversee the Flamingo's progress and that responsibility was assigned.

In short time, Siegel took the responsibility to heart and became immersed in the project.

Siegel's vision was grand: imported Italian marble, lavish rooms, wall-to-wall carpeting, a giant pool, the best food, and top-notch entertainment. As far as he was concerned, the Flamingo was going to be the biggest, most glamorous establishment in America.

However, with Siegel overseeing the construction of the Flamingo, the costs of the project skyrocketed, along with the concerns of his associates. As the price of the Flamingo increased, so too did Ben's assurances to his old friends that once they saw the fruits of their investment, their anxieties would be put at ease. Rumors of skimming surfaced but Meyer Lansky's assurances to Charlie Luciano seemed to dispel any purported funding discrepancies, and while many claim that Siegel's "skim" of the construction funds lead to this ultimate demise, there were probably several factors that led to Siegel's death in 1947 and not just the skimming of the construction funds (if there had been any). In the end, the organization decided to give their six-million-dollar investment a chance to develop, with the firm resolve that if the Flamingo failed, Benjamin Siegel would need to be retired.

The Flamingo opened on December 26, 1946, and for the first two days of its existence, the casino flourished. A headline group of entertainers, including Jimmy Durante, Xavier Cougat, and Rose Marie, performed to large crowds of Hollywood's top actors and actresses. It was a grand time for Siegel and the Flamingo. It appeared as if his vision in the desert was going to pay tremendous dividends.

After the casino's initial success, however, it began losing money; a lot of money. Without a doubt, the Flamingo was the grandest attraction in Las Vegas, but it was not an attractive outlet for regular gamblers. The locals still preferred to do their gaming business at the more down-to-earth casinos, such as the El Cortez and the El Rancho.

After a short period of time, the Flamingo closed its doors. The official line was that the hotel needed to finish construction. The bottom line was that Siegel had to find a way to stop losing money.

His problem was two-fold, a lack of local interest and questionable employees. Siegel had been duped. His employees were fixing games, top-stacking wins, and doing anything and everything in their power to take as much money from the house as possible.

Siegel quickly fixed his initial problems, and after bringing in a new crew of workers, developed a marketing concept to bring in the locals. Much to Bugsy's relief, when the Flamingo opened its doors for the second time, the club started to generate consistent profits.

In May of 1947, the Flamingo "reported" a profit of approximately $350,000.00 – This was what was reported, so the actual take could have been much more.

Despite the Flamingo's growing success, Ben Siegel had somehow some how angered the only person who could have ordered Siegel's murder – Charlie Luciano.

There has always been the misconception that the failure of the Flamingo and Siegel's unwillingness to pay back the debts he owed led to his demise. The truth of the matter was it was probably a combination of things that Siegel was doing that got him killed.

Drugs, the wire-service, the horses, his relationship with Virginia Hill, his hostile takeover of the Flamingo from Wilkerson, the attention he was bring to himself, and his associates, due to his bold and brash behavior, the bottom-line is, no one can really say what the ultimate reason was that Ben Siegel was marked for death, but he was. And by May of 2017, plans were put in place to kill Bugsy Siegel.

Chapter Eighteen
The Patsy

W hen Jack Dragna received word that he being assigned to oversee the Siegel murder, he knew the situation presented him with a number of concerns.

"Meyer and Ben had been friends since they were small boys, which meant they shared a very strong bond," Nick Moretta once said. "Jack probably sensed there was a possibility that, even though the order to kill Siegel had been given on orders from Charlie Luciano, if Meyer ever discovered who pulled the trigger on his old friend, he would feel compelled to avenge Ben's death.

"Jack did have a reputation for being a boss willing to forfeit his own men, but as he came to understand the possible repercussions involved in the Siegel killing, his concerns about sacrificing one of his own grew. It was easy for Jack to make decisions that had serious repercussions on the people around him. He was hard-core *Cosa Nostra*."

While Jack Dragna was more famous for his failed attempts to kill mobster Mickey Cohn, make no mistake, he was the main man in Los Angeles for two decades and had the ability to be a ruthless killer. In regards to the Siegel killing, however, Dragna concluded his family's involvement in the mechanics of the hit had to be distanced, and the triggerman had to be expendable. Enter Bob MacDonald.

"I probably had as much to do with Bob getting involved in the Siegel killing as anyone," Nick Moretta once confessed. "Gaynell and I had had Jack over for dinner. The next thing I know, all Gaynell and I were doing was bitching about Bob.

"Bob was into Jack for a pretty good chunk of change, about $25,000, again. Jack probably would have let Bob float on the money if we had asked him to, but when Gaynell mentioned Bob had slapped Betty Ann around again, he got pissed.

"After dinner, we went out to the back porch to smoke a cigar and have some brandy. Jack was unusually quiet. A few minutes passed, then he looked at me and asked what we were going to do about Bob.

"I chuckled and said the only way my problem was going to get solved was if someone killed the son-of-a-bitch. Jack took a drag on his smoke, threw down a shot of whiskey, and said, 'Maybe we should just have the prick killed.'

"He laughed and then told me to arrange a meeting between him and Bob. The grace period on Bob's debt was over, Jack stated, and it was time for Bob to make good on what he owed."

* * * * *

Bob MacDonald was nervous about the meeting with Dragna. With no prospects of paying Jack back the money he owed him, he knew he was in trouble.

Dragna had asked Bob to meet him at a downtown bar at 10:00 in the morning. Bob arrived at 9:45, Dragna at 10:30. Much to Bob's surprise, when Dragna sat by Bob's side, he greeted Bob with a warm smile and a handshake. After some idle chitchat, Dragna got down to business.

"You owe me twenty-five grand," Jack said. "I need to know how you intend to pay me."

Bob's brain scrambled to find the words for an answer that would appease Los Angeles' most powerful gangster but came up empty.

"I have an option for you," Dragna said. "The choice is yours, but if you say no, I'll expect my money by the end of the week, or I'll have someone put a bullet in your head. Understand?"

Bob nodded his head and listened as Jack Dragna provided him with an alternative way of paying back the money he owed. Dragna needed a person without ties to his organization to make a hit on a long-time associate of the Dragna family. Dragna told Bob if he agreed to do the hit, once the task was complete, he would be free of his debt.

While Bob MacDonald may have taken a while to ponder the offer, the reality of his situation was that he had no options. There was no way he could come up with twenty-five dollars, let alone twenty-five thousand dollars. Bob MacDonald had to either kill or be killed. Jack Dragna could not have fallen into a better situation, nor could Bob MacDonald have found himself involved in anything worse.

*****

Bob MacDonald had a fascination with guns. He owned a sizeable collection of handguns, but nothing that could be used to assassinate a target from afar. For the job he was going to do for Dragna, he needed a weapon that would be reliable, fast, efficient, and untraceable.

From his army experience, MacDonald knew the best weapon for assuring a kill was a carbine rifle. While he did not have a carbine, he did know someone who did. MacDonald remembered that Robert Hull had brought several weapons back from Germany with him at the end of the war. As a mess sergeant, the contacts Robert made were vast. Thus, Hull was able to secure delivery of war booty from Germany to his mother-in-law's home in Southern California with few problems.

"Getting weapons and souvenirs back into the States was an easy enough task," Robert Hull once said. "Everyone had to eat, and it was amazing how many friends I made by simply throwing an extra helping on a food tray or providing someone with a hot cup of coffee late at night. I especially took care of the guys in supply. When the time came to ship some things home, I didn't have a problem. From the second lieutenants all the way down the enlisted ranks, those guys remembered I had taken care of them in the chow line, and when I asked to have some personal items sent back home to California, it wasn't an issue."

At MacDonald's insistence, Betty Ann invited Marion and Robert Hull over to the house for lunch and a swim. The Hulls arrived at the MacDonald home at 822 Warner Avenue around eleven o'clock. The house was located less than a half-mile west of the Beverly Hills Country Club and just north of Wilshire, in a very affluent neighborhood.

"After lunch, Bob and I began talking about our experiences during the war," Hull recalled. "I told him how funny it felt for me to carry a weapon down Wilshire Boulevard during the early part of the war. It was at this point that Bob shifted the conversation to my carbine."

"Bob said Nick had told him I had kept my rifle and had also picked up a few other weapons while overseas. I shared with Bob that I had an Italian rifle, a Luger, and another rifle.

"Bob stated that he wished he could have gotten his weapon back home. I told him that after feeding the men in supply extra portions of food for several months, getting contraband shipped back home was one of the perks of the job.

"After a little more chit-chat, he asked if he could buy my guns from me. Since I had no real need for them, I offered them to Bob at no cost. He jumped on the suggestion, and the next thing I knew, we were off to Lawndale where I had the guns stored in Flossy's garage.

"Bob's demeanor that day was pleasant," Hull continued. "In my previous encounters with him, he'd always seemed very stand-offish and uppity. During the entire time in the car, Bob was actually very friendly and seemed to be relaxed."

After picking up the guns and returning to Los Angeles, MacDonald insisted on treating Robert and Marion to dinner at a swank Beverly Hills restaurant. Later, the two couples returned to the MacDonald house and spent the evening in conversation.

"This was the first time Bob was ever really a part of a conversation," Marion said. "In the past, he always had other things to do, was on his way out, or just kept to himself. This time, however, he was engaging, laughing, and seemed to be having a good time. At the end of the evening, Bob and Betty Ann walked us out, and as I went to get in the car, Bob hugged me good-night, then opened my car door for me. I was in shock."

The Hulls hoped Bob's behavior that night was a sign of a change within him that meant better days were ahead. As they would later come to learn, their hopes were to be unrealized.

Chapter Nineteen
The Week of the Siegel Killing

June 14, 1947

B ob MacDonald received word from Jack Dragna that their arrangement had been put into motion. Dragna told Bob he should expect several guests in the next few days. A short time later, a nanny arrived at the MacDonald house.

Frances was a well-dressed woman, perfectly manicured, and very beautiful. Ironically, Betty Ann had known this woman for much of her life. Frances was the wife of Jack Dragna.

"When Betty Ann told me Frances Dragna was at the house to help Mrs. Baker with the kids, she did so with a chuckle," Marion said. "Things had gotten to the point with Bob's gambling that Betty Ann first thought Frances was in the house to keep an eye on Bob and make sure he didn't run like he did at the start of World War II.

"While the thought that Bob had gotten himself into so much trouble that someone needed to watch him was upsetting, Frances was a nice enough lady and she was good company for Constance, so Betty Ann didn't raise a stink."

June 17, 1947

Betty Ann entered the front door with several bags. She had taken Marion out for a morning of shopping and lunch, the result of which was a few new outfits for her son, now almost six, and her one-year-old daughter.

"Hello?" Betty Ann said as she entered the house.

"Up here, Mrs. MacDonald," Constance yelled from the upstairs landing.

"Hello, Constance. Did my mother come by?"

"She and Mr. Moretta were here a while ago," Constance said.

"Great." Betty Ann set the bags down onto the floor. "Did they say what time they wanted me to meet them?"

"Five," Constance said, heading downstairs. "They want to take you and the kids out to dinner."

Betty Ann's attention had shifted to the dining room, where an enormous floral arrangement and fruit basket sat on the table.

"Mr. MacDonald's war buddies brought them," Constance said. She pointed into the backyard, where Bob and three men stood talking by the pool.

"War buddies?" Betty Ann responded.

"They say they're here on business."

Bob spotted Betty Ann standing in the dining room. "Hey, Honey," he said, as he opened the sliding glass door, "I want you to meet some of my buddies from Germany."

"Hello, Mrs. MacDonald," one of the men said, approaching Betty Ann and extending his hand. "My name is Gus, and these gentlemen are my associates, Frank and Eddie."

Betty Ann guardedly took the man's hand.

"Gus Jackson," he said with a smile.

She studied Gus for a moment, and then looked at Frank and Eddie. She had seen men of a similar type before. After all, Nick was Italian, and one thing about Italian men is that they have a very distinct look. With Frances Dragna in the house, Betty Ann knew the men were probably tied to Jack, so they were more than likely in the same business, and they were there for the same reason, to keep an eye on Bob. But why were there *three* of them?

"I suppose I have you, gentlemen, to thank for the gifts?" Betty Ann said.

"It's the least we could do," Gus said. "I know how my wife reacts to unannounced house guests."

Everybody chuckled except Betty Ann, particularly after Bob announced that the men would probably be staying with them for a few days.

"I haven't had a chance to meet many of Bob's marine friends," Betty Ann said, forcing a smile. "I hope we get an opportunity to visit. I would love to hear about some of your experiences together, especially the ones about Okinawa."

"We'll have to put an evening aside for that, Mrs. MacDonald," Eddie offered.

Gus shifted his eyes to Eddie, clearly agitated that he had spoken. He glanced back at Betty Ann and realized she was onto them.

"We'll try not to be any trouble, Mrs. MacDonald," he said.

Betty Ann produced a softer smile and then asked Mrs. Baker to show the men to their rooms. After they'd gone upstairs, she turned her attention to Bob.

"Your war buddies don't even know you were in the army and not the marines, or that you were in Europe and not the Pacific. Care to tell me what the hell is going on?"

Bob merely lowered his head and stared at the ground.

"You're into something you have no business in, aren't you?"

Bob kept his eyes locked on the ground. Betty Ann waited a moment for a response, then realized one wasn't going to be coming anytime soon, so she returned to the bags in the foyer, collected her morning purchases, and went upstairs.

"I knew something wasn't kosher," Betty Ann would tell Marion. "Later, when I asked Gus what business he was in, he forced a smile and said he and his associates represented a private organization. They were on the West Coast looking for new opportunities and thought Bob could help facilitate a meeting with the Hughes people. It was such BS. The only thing that prevented me from getting all pissy was I suspected Bob was the cause of all this and not our visitors. They were probably just doing their jobs."

* * * * *

For the next few days, Bob and the boys were inseparable. If Bob went out, one of his friends went with him. If Bob sat by the pool, one of his friends went with him. If Bob went to the bathroom, one of his friends went with him.

Betty Ann merely accepted the men as a part of her life. She didn't question why they were in her home, what they wanted, or when they were going to leave. She went about her business. As far as Bob was concerned, and the trouble he was in, Betty Ann simply didn't care anymore; it was too hurtful and took too much energy.

Chapter Twenty
Goodbye, Benny

June 20, 1947

Betty Ann opened the front door and entered her house. As she did, she heard the phone on the kitchen counter ringing. She picked up the receiver and heard a very short conversation.

"They just settled in for dinner," one voice said.

"I'll send 'em now, so they can get in place," said the other voice, which Betty Ann recognized as Gus's.

Both parties hung up. Within a few seconds, Bob, Gus, and Eddie appeared on the upstairs landing. As the men descended the stairs, Betty Ann noticed that Bob was carrying a duffle bag with the name R.J. Hull stenciled on the side. Bob made his way to the front door, set the duffle bag onto the floor, and then looked at his wife with concern.

"Where are you going?" Betty Ann asked.

Bob walked to Betty Ann and engulfed her in a bear-like embrace. It was the first time in quite a while that she'd felt some sincerity while being held by her husband.

"Just let me do what I have to do," Bob said.

Eddie picked up the duffle bag and exited the house. "Time to go," Gus said to Bob.

"Where is my husband going?" Betty Ann asked.

"Bob," Gus said, ignoring Betty Ann's question, "time to go!"

Bob kissed Betty Ann on the cheek, then hustled out the front door and got into the car with Eddie.

"Where is my husband going?" Betty Ann snapped at Gus.

Gus remained mute.

"I asked you a goddamn question, Gus, or whatever the hell your name is," Betty Ann said as she approached the front door. "Where is my husband going?"

Gus waited until Eddie's car had backed out of the driveway, pulled into the street, and disappeared down the street. "Let things play out, Mrs. MacDonald," he said softly. "I know this is confusing, but everything will be over in a short while. Maybe after tonight, things will get better for you and your children."

A clattering from the upstairs landing broke the moment. Betty Ann looked up to see Frank making his way clumsily down the stairs with the luggage.

"You gonna give me a hand with these," Frank barked, "or are you just going to stand there?"

Gus kept his eyes and warm smile locked on Betty Ann, providing Frank with the answer to his question.

"Thanks for nothin'," Frank quipped, as he made his way through the foyer, past Gus, and out the door.

Betty couldn't speak.

"Thank you for your hospitality," Gus said with a tip of his hat. "You've been a perfect hostess."

With that, Gus exited the house, leaving Betty Ann standing at the doorway, wondering what was going on. While a million thoughts were racing through her mind, Bob going out to murder one of America's most feared gangsters probably wasn't one of them.

* * * * *

On the last day of his life, Ben Siegel left the Flamingo Hotel and Casino for the airport in Las Vegas. When Bugsy and his friend Swifty Morgan boarded Western Airlines Flight 23 for Los Angeles, it was 12:53 a.m.

After Siegel and Morgan arrived in Los Angeles, Bugsy called for a taxicab. The dapper, forty-two-year-old New York native was driven to the Beverly Hills residence of Miss Virginia Hill, his mistress. The two men arrived at Hill's home at approximately 2:30 a.m.

As Siegel and Smiley entered the house, Charles "Chick" Hill, Virginia's brother, and Jerri Mason, Chick's fiancée and Virginia's personal secretary, greeted them. Virginia Hill had taken a trip to Paris, France, leaving Chick and Jerri to house-sit during her absence. After a brief exchange of pleasantries, everyone went to their respective upstairs bedrooms and went to sleep.

In the morning, Siegel had breakfast with Swifty, Chick, and Jerri. After eating, he used the downstairs phone to call his friend, Alan Smiley. Siegel asked Smiley to serve as his driver for a day of errands. Smiley was eager to accommodate his request and told Ben he would be over in an hour or so.

Siegel then went upstairs and made several "private" phone calls. Handling business over the phone was not an uncommon occurrence for Siegel. On this day, however, Ben seemed to make a great many more calls than usual.

When Smiley arrived at the house, he had a quick cup of coffee, and then he and Ben headed to the Brentwood home of Mickey Cohen, another one of Bugsy's notorious friends.

Before Siegel, Cohen had been a small-time bookmaker, working out of a paint store. After Bugsy brought the bulldog-looking thug into his operation to serve as his private bodyguard, Cohen's status was upgraded. In fact, he was now conducting business on Sunset Boulevard.

On most occasions, Cohen never failed to grab an opportunity to spend time with Siegel. On this day, however, when Bugsy asked his friend to accompany him while he did his errands and then have dinner with him and Smiley that evening, Cohen declined, claiming to have a multitude of things to do that day.

While much speculation has been given to whether or not Cohen had knowledge of Siegel's impending doom, there is no evidence to support those claims. Several years after Siegel's killing, Cohen recalled that his final conversation with Bugsy was "uneventful." Cohen did, however, say that "Bennie seemed exceptionally nervous about something, but nothing he wanted to discuss. If he knew anything at all about a contract out on his life, he never shared that information with me."

After chatting with Cohen, Siegel went to the home of George Raft. The two men visited for a while, chatting about a number of non-eventful situations. Siegel invited Raft to dinner that night. Under most circumstances, Raft probably would have accepted Siegel's offer. However, the famous movie star had an early-morning shoot and declined Bugsy's invitation.

Siegel and Smiley returned to Beverly Hills, where Siegel took in a haircut, a shave, and a manicure at Drucker's Barbershop. After his grooming session at Drucker's, Siegel walked to the office of his attorney, Joe Ross, for an afternoon meeting.

His discussion with Ross that day was not unlike his conversations with his attorney on most other days. It involved the Flamingo Hotel and Casino. According to Ross, while Bugsy was concerned about a few of the financial aspects of his business dealings, in general, he did not seem overly concerned about too much of anything.

After about an hour with the attorney, Siegel and Smiley returned to 810 North Linden Drive. It was approximately four o'clock in the afternoon.

Siegel told Smiley to return to the house at 7:30 so that he, Siegel, could take Smiley, Chick, and Jerri out for dinner. There was a new restaurant Siegel had heard about called Jack's Café, located in Ocean Park, and he was eager to try it out. After Smiley left, Siegel visited with Chick and Jerri for a while and then spent the next few hours on the phone.

At 7:30 sharp, Smiley returned to the Hill home and picked up Siegel, Chick, and Jerri. By eight o'clock, the group was enjoying a peaceful meal. During dinner, Siegel seemed especially pleased about the progress of the Flamingo Hotel and Casino, his six-million-dollar Las Vegas project.

* * * * *

Eddie headed south on Warner. After traveling two blocks, he turned left on Wilshire Boulevard; then after passing the Beverly Hills Country Club, he made a left on North Linden. As Bob looked about, he knew where he was; this was the same neighborhood that Howard Hughes had crashed his IF-11 aircraft in, less than a year before. MacDonald grew nervous as Eddie shut the lights off, slowed his car, and began calling out house numbers.

"802...804...806," Eddie mumbled as he pulled the car to a stop at 806 North Linden. "There it is; up there, 810 North Linden."

Bob sat in disbelief. The journey he and Eddie had taken required a 1.8-mile drive and about four minutes.

Eddie shut off the engine, and then looked at Bob. "Get the guns outta the trunk," he said.

Bob hesitated.

"Look! If you're having second thoughts," Eddie whispered, "get over em'." He opened his jacket pocket and revealed a revolver he had in his waistband. "If you don't do this, my instructions are to do the job myself, then put a bullet in your head, too."

Bob wanted to run, but his feet wouldn't move.

"Get out of the car," Eddie ordered again. "Let's get the guns and get set up."

Bob opened his door and got out of the car. He stood by the side of the vehicle, his knees quivering. Eddie went to the back of the car, popped open the trunk, and stared at the duffle bag.

The bags were unzipped and each man produced a weapon. Bob took a .30 caliber rifle and Eddie was probably holding a .45 caliber machine gun.

With Eddie in the lead, the two men crept up the driveway at 808 North Linden. The two homes were separated by a wooden latticework fence, which provided Bob and Eddie excellent cover from the residents of the white mansion at 810 North Linden. They positioned themselves in the shrubbery.

"Just rest easy," Eddie said. "This could take a while."

Bob glanced at his watch. It read 8:45.

As time passed, Eddie and Bob smoked a number of cigarettes. There was no conversation between the two, just an exchange of several smokes. Over the course of the next two hours, a number of cars drove up and down North Linden, but it wasn't until approximately 10:40 PM that one captured Eddie's attention.

"This could be them," he said, as he spotted a car, that seemed to fit the type and color he was looking for.

As the vehicle pulled into the drive at 810 North Linden, Bob's heart began racing a hundred miles an hour as he anticipated his task at hand. He took out his weapon, a 30-caliber carbine rifle, and gripped it tightly in his hand.

Four people exited the car and made their way into the house. After a few seconds, the lights in the foyer went on.

* * * * *

Around nine o'clock, Siegel and his friends finished their meal, left Jack's Café, and were headed home. When Smiley reached Beverly Hills, Siegel had him stop at the Beverly Wilshire Drugstore. Siegel wanted to purchase some camphor oil, which is used to soften tight, aching muscles.

When the group arrived at the Hill home, Chick and Jerri excused themselves to the upstairs bedroom, while Smiley and Siegel adjourned to the living room. Siegel and Smiley sat on the sofa. Smiley was positioned closest to the window, while Siegel sat at the far end of the couch.

Siegel had taken a copy of the *Los Angeles Examiner* from Jack's Café. As he flipped open the newspaper, an advertisement, posted on a small piece of paper, fell to the ground. He bent over and picked up the tiny advertisement; *Good-night; Sleep Well—Compliments of Jack's*. Siegel chuckled at the advertisement, set the piece of paper on the coffee table, and began reading the newspaper.

* * * * *

From their position, Bob could see into the living room of the 810 North Linden home, but the curtains obstructed most of his view.

Bob raised his weapon and carefully rested the barrel of the rifle on the latticework. The end of the barrel shook slightly as he tried to line up the cross-hairs on the living room window, a mere ten feet away.

* * * * *

As they entered front room of the house, Smiley flipped on the lights; illuminating the room. He asked Siegel if he wanted a drink. Siegel declined. Smiley decided to pour himself one.

* * * * *

While the drapes of the window were barely open, they were open enough for Bob to see inside the room.

The room was lit, and Bob had a view into the home. Eddie searched the room for a moment.

"You want the one on the couch," he said, identifying MacDonald's target. "He's the one we want." He picked up the other weapon. "Don't fuck this thing up," he said.

One can only imagine the thoughts that were running through Bob's head at that moment.

Had life become this bad?

Was this the only way out?

What were his options?

Who was the man he was going to kill?

Bob hesitated briefly, then locked the crosshairs of his weapon onto the head of his victim. Compared to his experience in Aachen, Germany, this should have been easy. His target was unsuspecting and sat a mere twelve feet away. But, despite the proximity of his victim, Bob knew this wasn't like Aachen. This wasn't war. This was murder.

Bob hesitated for a final moment. One last chance to run; but then, where would he hide? He took a deep, gathering breath, placed the victim's head in his sights, then allowed his finger to squeeze the trigger of the 30-caliber carbine rifle he held in his hands.

* * * * *

The first shot rang out, and within a few seconds, nine shots were fired into the home. Four bullets hit their mark.

Siegel was hit in the head twice. The first shot hit Bugsy's right cheek and exited through the left side of his neck. His vertebra was shattered, causing his head to snap back onto the couch.

The second bullet entered Siegel's right eye and exited through his left. Police would later discover a portion of his eyelid about ten feet away from his body.

Two more slugs would hit Siegel in the chest. Another bullet nicked the coat sleeve on Smiley's left arm, while another shot shattered a small marble figure of Bacchus that sat on Virginia Hill's piano. Another slug shattered a painting of a nude holding a wine glass, while two other shots embedded themselves in the wall of the home, creating holes the size of silver dollars.

* * * * *

When Bob stopped his shooting, he looked into the house and saw the man slumped back on the couch. MacDonald had completed his part of the arrangement.

The sound of a car being started captured his attention.

Eddie hit the gas pedal, and the car quickly moved up North Linden and away from the murder site.

According to the plan, Bob was now on foot. He ran to the west toward the Los Angeles Country Club.

A million thoughts were running through Bob MacDonald's mind as he crossed the golf course headed toward his home about a mile away; *who was the man that he had just murdered? Why did he have to be killed? And most importantly, why, oh dear God, why did he, Robert Crosbie MacDonald, agree to commit such a gruesome deed?*

* * * * *

Betty Ann was asleep when Bob slithered into their bedroom, and while not remembering the exact time her husband came in that evening, she did remember that Bob's rustling about in the closet woke her.

"I sat up and asked Bob if he was alright," Betty Ann said. "He rambled something incoherent, then left the room.

"It was the middle of the night, and Bob was leaving," Betty Ann recalled. "I realized things hadn't changed at all, so I rolled over, pulled the blanket over my shoulders, and fell back asleep."

* * * * *

Twenty minutes after the shooting, Moe Sedway, Gus Greenbaum, and three henchmen marched into the lobby of the Flamingo Hotel and Casino in Las Vegas, Nevada. At barely five feet tall, Sedway was a Mob runt. On his own merit, he would not have gathered much respect. However, when standing next to Greenbaum, the well-known frontman of Meyer Lansky and the head of Luciano's gambling venture in Tucson, "Little Moe" captured everyone's attention when he announced there had been a change in the management of the Flamingo Hotel.

"As of this moment, we control the Flamingo Hotel," he announced to the patrons and staff.

"Ben Siegel owns the Flamingo," one of the pit bosses replied.

Greenbaum chuckled, then produced a knowing smile. "Not anymore," he said. "Ben Siegel is dead!"

For a brief moment, the crowd seemed stunned. Then, without missing a spin of the wheel on the roulette table or a roll of the dice at the craps table, the games of chance resumed.

Captain W.W. White of the Beverly Hills Police Department later stated that Siegel was killed at approximately 10:50 PM. Siegel's killer left nine spent, 30-caliber, U.S. Army carbine shells at the crime scene. While his department had few clues to work with, Captain White was confident that the killer would be found.

On a side-note, there has been some speculation that Allen Smiley, Siegel's longtime friend, was involved in setting up Siegel for his execution. This makes no sense. If this were true, why would Smiley take a seat on the couch in close proximity to Siegel? Would anyone really trust a shooter to be that accurate with their shots?

Chapter Twenty-One
Aftermath of Murder

Betty Ann awoke early. As she came downstairs, she noticed Bob was sleeping on the living room couch. An empty bottle of whiskey lay on the floor next to him.

She considered waking him to ask what had happened the night before but decided to leave him alone. If Bob wanted to share what had transpired, he would. If not, she was done worrying about his bizarre behavior. Her home was hers once again. Bob's friends were gone, and so too was Frances Dragna.

When Betty Ann entered the kitchen, she found a pot of coffee and the morning paper waiting for her, compliments of Constance Baker. She poured herself a cup, then went into the back yard where she began reading by the pool.

She opened the *Los Angeles Herald* and saw a picture of Benjamin Siegel. The headlines read "Gangster, Benjamin Siegel Murdered." A strange feeling struck Betty Ann, and for a moment her imagination ran wild. Was Bob involved in this killing? Was that what his recent strange behavior was all about? The men in her home, who were they, really? Why was Frances Dragna, the wife of LA's most powerful mobster, a five-day houseguest?

"Can I warm your cup," Constance said, interrupting Betty Ann's thoughts.

"Please."

"Did you see where Bugsy Siegel was murdered last night?" Constance asked.

"You don't think…?" Betty Ann stopped herself, and then looked to Constance to complete the sentence.

Constance leaned down and embraced Betty Ann from behind. "I'd like to think not," she said.

Betty Ann forced a meek smile.

After she finished reading the paper, Betty Ann returned to the upstairs bathroom and took a long, hot shower. Just as she stepped out of the tub, she heard Bob bellowing from downstairs for the newspaper. She stepped from the bedroom to the upstairs landing and told Bob the paper was outside on the patio table. By the time she'd thrown on a pair of shorts and a top and come downstairs, Bob had left.

"Mr. MacDonald is gone," Constance stated. "He looked nervous."

"Great," Betty Ann said. "Not a day has passed and we're back to business as usual."

* * * * *

Bob's behavior before the Siegel killing may have been strange, but after the gangster's slaying, his conduct became intolerable.

"In the weeks following the Siegel murder, Bob's demeanor went from bad to worse," Gaynell recalled. "He was consumed with enormous paranoia. Betty Ann said Bob was constantly pacing the house and looking out the windows, acting as if someone was coming to get him."

"No one knew what was wrong with Bob," Marion said. "The term 'battle fatigue' was thrown out a few times. I think everyone sensed the changes in his behavior were caused by something more significant than his war experiences. In the back of our minds, we all knew something was wrong. We didn't know what, but we knew there was something that just wasn't right."

"When Betty Ann first read about the Siegel killing, she suspected Bob was involved," Gaynell once said. "To what extent, she was unsure, but as time passed she began to believe more and more that his behavior change was a result of his having somehow been a part of it."

By late July, the demons in Bob MacDonald's life were in complete control. In addition to his return to gambling, heavy drinking, and women, marijuana and cocaine were complementing his recreational activities.

* * * * *

In early August, Betty Ann returned home after spending a day of shopping with Ella MacDonald. She entered the living room, looked through the sliding glass door into the backyard, and saw Bob having sex with another woman on the pool deck. Her initial reaction was one of fury. Almost immediately, however, Betty Ann's anger subsided, and her emotions were replaced by a sense of nothingness.

"I pulled open the sliding glass door, and Bob looked at me," Betty Ann recalled. "I thought maybe he would have stopped fucking the woman he was with, but he didn't. Instead, he just gave me a blank gaze and continued about his business. That is until Ella stepped outside and stood beside me."

Shortly after that incident, Bob MacDonald, at the urging of his father, consented to seek treatment for the addictions that were consuming his life and admitted himself to the Sawtell Veterans Hospital.

"Archie begged Betty Ann to stay with Bob," Marion said. "Archie felt that, for the sake of the children, Betty Ann had to try one more time to make the marriage work. Archie promised Betty Ann that, if Bob did not become a responsible family man and father, he was going to be cut out of the family and therefore the family money."

Grudgingly, Betty Ann agreed to stay in the marriage. She told Archie her children were her world, and that her love from that day forward would be strictly for them.

* * * * *

"Betty Ann always suspected Bob's extreme swing in behavior centered on the Siegel murder," Gaynell once said. "But she never actually heard Bob confess to having been involved in the crime until September of 1947."

For Bob and Betty Ann, verbal confrontations were a daily occurrence. It was during one of those tirades that Bob confessed to his spouse his participation in the Siegel killing.

"Betty Ann and Bob were arguing over Bob's lack of employment," Gaynell once said. "Bob began to attack her verbally, then suddenly he started crying. He sobbed uncontrollably for several minutes.

"Bob finally gathered himself and simply stated he was the one who had killed Siegel. Betty Ann said she went completely numb.

"Deep down," Gaynell continued, "Betty Ann was hoping the underlying cause of Bob's inexplicable behavior was due to another affair, his on-going gambling problems, or as some people were speculating, a suppressed war memory."

At the Sawtell Medical Facility in Downtown Los Angeles, Bob's doctors were trying to get him to admit his deepest, darkest secret to a family member. By making his secrets known, they told him, he would free his torment and only then could he get better. It seemed to work, especially since, after his confession to Betty Ann, Bob's secret was no longer a burden he carried alone; for a brief period of time, he seemed at ease.

The confession had the opposite effect on Betty Ann. She knew that her situation was much worse than she had ever fathomed. She now feared for her life and for the lives of her children.

"When Betty Ann told me Bob was involved in the Siegel murder, I was shocked but not surprised," Gaynell said. "Hearing that news gave me the ability to support Betty Ann in her move to leave Bob, something I should have done long before I learned that Bob was a murderer."

Betty Ann went to Archie MacDonald.

"I'm sure Archie reacted to learning of Bob's involvement in the Siegel matter much as I did," Gaynell said. "Neither one of us knew exactly what to do, but we knew we had to do something."

Archie had an advantage over Gaynell. As the guardian of the wealthiest man in the world, he had had experience in handling scandalous situations such as this one.

September 7, 1947

At Bob's insistence, Betty Ann invited Marion and Robert Hull to the house for dinner. While Bob's request seemed unusual, Betty Ann wanted things to look as if it were business as usual, so she invited the Hulls to her home.

"I remember that night very well," Marion said. "Betty Ann seemed to be a bit on edge, which was totally against her nature. Bob, on the other hand, was chatty, witty, and relaxed, which was highly unusual for him."

As the evening progressed, the conversation covered a great many topics. Then Bob and Robert began to talk about their experiences in Europe. Bob asked Robert if he'd like to go into the family room for a cigar and a brandy. Robert accepted, and the two men left their wives and headed into the other room.

"After taking a drink, Bob looked me dead in the eye and told me he had killed Siegel," Robert said. "He chuckled, but it wasn't a chuckle in jest, it was more of disbelief. Then, he took a deep breath, shook his head and began to cry.

"After he gathered himself, he shared with me some of the details of the crime, told me that Jack Dragna had made him the deal to clear his markers and how his life was being consumed. Bob said his hope was that someone would find out what he had done and do something about it."

While Bob was confessing to Hull his involvement in the Siegel killing, in the other room, Betty Ann was revealing to Marion that she was going to leave her husband. Marion had known about Bob's adultery for years, and she had seen the results of the beatings Betty Ann had taken, so she was relieved to hear that Betty Ann was going to end her marriage.

"Betty Ann asked me to keep quiet through the weekend," Marion said. "She seemed to have her reasons for not wanting anyone to know what she was doing, so I agreed not to tell anyone, not even my husband."

Marion stayed silent. Tragically, so did Robert Hull.

"Driving home that night, I wanted to tell Marion what Bob had said, but I didn't," Robert said. "A thousand thoughts were running through my mind. I didn't know if I should tell the police, tell Gaynell, tell Nick, or what.

"I knew if I went to the authorities I could be putting the entire family in danger. The other thing was that Bob seemed so nonchalant about his confession. I wasn't sure if he was serious or not. I didn't know Bob all that well, so in the back of my mind, I was thinking maybe this was all just a bad joke.

"I had selfish reasons for not going to the police right away, as well," Robert confessed. "I wasn't sure what ramifications I was going to suffer, especially since if Bob did kill Siegel, the gun he had used was one of the guns I had given him."

As a result of his fears, Hull decided to ponder his options. It was a decision that haunted him for the remainder of his life.

By September 12, 1947, Betty Ann had put in place all the pieces necessary to leave Bob MacDonald.

"Betty Ann went to the cardinal of the Catholic Church in Los Angeles," Gaynell once said. "As she began telling the cardinal of Bob's infidelity, his beatings of her, his gambling problems, his drinking, and his drug addictions, the cardinal interrupted.

"'In matters of marriage,' the Cardinal stated, 'one must remain tolerant and understanding. The Catholic Church believes in working through difficulties; this is an important aspect of the faith. Only under the most extreme conditions would a divorce be considered.'

"Betty Ann proceeded to provide the cardinal with a few more specifics of her situation," Gaynell continued. "While I don't know what she shared with him, I do know that when she left his office, her request for an annulment had been granted."

Later that same day, Betty Ann called on her attorney, Birger Tinglof. During her conversation with Tinglof, she asked that a new last will and testament be drawn up. Betty Ann named the MacDonalds' two children as sole beneficiaries of her entire net worth, which was approximately $100,000. The new will also stated that Bob was to receive nothing.

Betty Ann returned home that evening to find Constance with the children. Bob was nowhere to be seen, a welcome discovery at that point. Betty Ann spent the evening with her children, made a phone call to her mother, and seemed to be excited about the prospects for her future.

Later that night, Bob returned home. His evening had been spent on women, drinking, and gambling. He managed to reach the couch before he collapsed.

Betty Ann refused to make a fuss or confront her husband over where he had been, whom he had slept with, or how much money he had lost. She didn't care anymore. She knew her life with Mac-Donald was over, and in the morning, Bob would know as well. Betty Ann MacDonald went to bed that evening believing that the future for her and her children was going to bring wonderful things.

Chapter Twenty-Two
The Nightmare Revisited

September 13, 1947

After Bob MacDonald killed Betty Ann, he looked to the doorway of the bedroom and saw his six-year-old son. It mattered not to Bob the ramifications for those he was going to leave behind, so he placed the barrel of the rifle into his mouth, ignored the pleas of his child, then pulled the trigger of the weapon, ending his life.

Constance Baker grabbed the MacDonald child just as the third shot sounded. Not knowing the full extent of what was going on; she had one thing in mind, to get herself and the boy to safety. Constance held the child as tightly to her body as possible, and the child began to cry.

"My daddy went 'pow,' and then his head was gone," the boy kept saying over and over again, between sobs. "My daddy went 'pow.'"

Constance placed the boy on the couch and covered him with a blanket. Dreading what she would find, she knew she had to return upstairs.

Betty Ann's body lay face down in the hallway, a few feet from the bedroom. The once small puddle of blood had grown into a large pool on the white carpet. The horror of the scene overtook Constance. Her body began to tremble. Her legs shook, causing her to slide to the floor where she cried uncontrollably.

After she gathered herself, she returned downstairs. While her heart told her to call the police immediately, Constance hesitated. She had worked for Gaynell and Betty Ann for over eight years. She knew how things needed to be. Both Gaynell Moretta and Archie MacDonald had to know about this horrible deed before the police were involved, especially with Bob's dramatic statement involving his participation in a murder.

Constance called the Moretta home. There was no answer. She then called the MacDonald home and reached Archie.

Upon hearing the news that his son had killed Betty Ann and then shot himself, Archie let out a gasp, which was followed by a moment of silence. Then Archibald MacDonald, the overseer of one of the most powerful men in the world, began to sob.

"It was a horrible situation," Constance once said. "Having to tell a parent that his child is dead is the worst thing in the world to have to do. My heart was broken already, but hearing Mr. MacDonald's pain made things even more tragic."

After Archie regained his composure, he asked Constance if she had called the police or Gaynell yet. Constance stated that she had tried to reach Gaynell, but had been unsuccessful.

Archie instructed her to keep trying to reach Mrs. Moretta, but not to call the police for at least ten minutes. Constance agreed. She called the Moretta home again, with the same result—no answer. Next, Constance called the home of Bob Rockwell, Betty Ann's brother, and Gaynell's son.

"I remember the sick feeling that instantly came over me when I received the call from Mrs. Baker," Bob Rockwell once said. "Betty Ann was my baby sister, and I loved her a great deal. I was devastated.

"Constance told me she had not yet been able to reach my mother, nor had she called the police. I knew my mother was out shopping that morning, and then she was meeting Betty Ann later that afternoon at Mom's house. I told Constance to call the police and that I was on my way."

J.F. Werner of the West Los Angeles Division of the Los Angeles Police Department was the first police officer to arrive on the scene, and shortly after that, Detective Christensen of the West Los Angeles Detective Division arrived as well. Upon entering the MacDonald home, the officers found Betty Ann dead in the upstairs hallway. She had been shot twice in the back. In the bedroom, they found Bob lying alongside the bed with a single gunshot wound to the head. In Bob's hands was the 30-caliber carbine rifle.

The officers asked the lone witness, Constance Baker, a series of questions concerning the incident. When Constance informed the officers that the MacDonalds were fighting just before the shooting and that the couple had been having marital problems, Detective Christensen wrote the information down on a notepad, ended the questioning, and called the coroner's office at 12:45 PM. Bob Rockwell arrived at Betty Ann's home at approximately 12:50 PM, and was asked by Officer Werner to identify the bodies.

Bob Rockwell: "Going into Betty Ann's home that day was the most dreadful thing I'd ever had to do in my life. I remember trying to walk up the stairs and having my legs go numb. They didn't want to work.

"I reached the upstairs landing and saw Betty Ann. *Oh sweet God almighty*, I thought to myself. There was my little sister, lying in a pool of blood, lifeless. She was gone. The numb feeling I had in my legs inundated my entire body. I stood there unable to breathe, unable to move, unable to think. The officer then asked me if the victim was Betty Ann. I couldn't talk, so I just nodded my head yes.

"The officer asked me if I could identify the second body as that of Bob MacDonald. I looked into the bedroom and saw Bob's body on the floor. I told the officer I thought it was Bob, but I couldn't be sure."

Bob MacDonald's features were unrecognizable. The muzzle of the gun had been pressed up against the roof of his mouth when the trigger was pulled, making positive identification almost impossible.

"The entire front of Bob's head was gone," Bob Rockwell continued. "I tried to ascertain if it was really him. I knew it was, but I honestly couldn't tell for sure. When the officer asked me to try again, I looked toward Bob's body and then nodded my head yes. 'It's him,' I told the officer.

Bob Rockwell returned downstairs, collected himself, and then decided to call the Moretta home in search of his mother. As the phone rang, Bob's heart raced. He knew he needed to find his mother before she arrived at the MacDonald home, later that afternoon. As the phone continued to ring, Bob Rockwell hoped his mother would pick up the line, but in a way, he was relieved with every passing ring that she didn't.

"How does a son tell his mother her daughter has been murdered?" Bob once said. "It was an experience I didn't want to have."

* * * * *

As Gaynell and Nick Moretta pulled into the drive of their home at 9644 Olympic Boulevard, they were not too concerned when they saw a police car parked along the curb in front of the house.

"I still had a number of friends with the Los Angeles Police Department, so it wasn't uncommon for some of the fellas to drop by from time to time," Gaynell said. "At first, I thought nothing of the police car sitting along the curb, but after we got out of the car and I noticed two officers I'd never seen before approaching, I realized this wasn't a social call.

"When the officer told me Betty Ann was dead, I lost it. I didn't remember how I got there, but the next thing I knew was I was at Betty Ann's house, and my son was holding me in his arms."

"Mom wanted to go into the house and see Betty Ann," Bob Rockwell said. "After being in the home and having to identify the bodies, I knew that was not what she needed."

After about ten minutes, Gaynell insisted on making a phone call. So police escorted her to the next-door neighbors' home and asked to use the phone. Gaynell promptly called Florence Clark, the person she always turned to in times of crisis.

* * * * *

"We had just gotten back from the Veterans Hospital in downtown Los Angeles," Marion said. "My little brother, Gene, had been working on the docks in San Pedro. A piece of machinery had fallen from a crate, hit him in the leg, and thrown him into the water. The wound was a compound fracture and was exposed to gasoline and oil in the water. After about a week, Gene developed a staph infection, which ended up putting him in the hospital for about three weeks.

"We had thought of dropping in on Betty Ann that morning. As we approached the cross street, however, I remembered she had mentioned she was taking her son to the dentist, so we decided to take Gene home to Moms instead. We had only been home for about ten minutes when the phone rang.

"'I'll get it,' Mom said, as she walked toward the phone. I remember my mother saying; 'Hello,' then watching an expression of pure dread consume her. When my mother's eyes shifted to me, she began to cry. I knew something horrible had happened. My heart began to pound against my chest, and I just knew the call was about Betty Ann."

"Gaynell was crying hysterically," Florence Clark once said. "I knew right away that something had happened. I knew with Renny, I knew with Ralph, but when Gaynell told me Betty Ann was dead, I didn't want to believe my ears.

"'Flossy, come quick,' Gaynell screamed. 'The son-of-a-bitch has killed my Betty Ann. Please, oh please, hurry.'

"Gaynell dropped the phone and began crying hysterically. Bob Rockwell came on the phone and said he would be taking his mother to her house, and we should meet them at her place as quickly as we could."

"After my mother hung up the phone," Marion recalled, "she immediately came to me and held me in her arms.

"'It's Betty Ann,' I said. 'Isn't it?'

"'Honey, I'm sorry,' my mother said.

"I cried hysterically for ten or fifteen minutes," Marion added. "After Mom and Gene were able to calm me a bit, I realized that the person I had grown up with, shared so many memories with, shared so many secrets with, and shared so many dreams with was gone. I began crying again; this time, however, my tears were more sorrowful. It was the worst day of my life.

"Gene stayed at home, while Mom and I drove to Gaynell and Nick's house. The ride took about half an hour, and neither my mother nor I said one single word. We were both too stunned to speak.

"When we arrived, there were a number of cars parked in the driveway and along the street. We had to park a good distance from the house, and as we walked up the sidewalk, a police officer approached us. 'Ladies,' the officer said, 'can I help you?' Mom explained who we were. The officer expressed his condolences and then escorted us to the house.

"When the front door opened, all I saw was a sea of faces. There were so many people. I didn't pay too much attention to who was there because everywhere I looked, my memories of my best friend flooded over me.

"Gaynell arrived about twenty minutes or so later. 'Where's Flossy?' she cried out as she entered the house. Gaynell ran to Mom as soon as she saw her and held her tightly in her arms. Then, she sobbed like a baby for a long, long time.

"As I watched my mother rock her best friend in her arms, I could see what a special relationship they had. The two of them shared such a wonderful bond, and despite the horror of the day, I could see their love for one another by the way my mother was trying to comfort her."

Over the course of the next hour, the Moretta home became a beehive of activity. Franklin Shaw, Joe Shaw, Ben Brown, the coroner, a number of police officers of various rank, and Jack Dragna all stopped in to pay their respects.

* * * * *

Gaynell had been snuggled in Florence's bosom for about thirty minutes before Nick approached her. The Moretta phone had been ringing non-stop, but with Nick screening calls, Gaynell was free to be with her thoughts. As Nick approached his wife, however, it was clear that this was a caller she'd want to talk with.

"It's Archie," Nick said.

"I'll take it in the bedroom," Gaynell replied.

She sprang to her feet and hurried to the back of the house so she could have more privacy. Nick went back to the phone in the kitchen, and as soon as Gaynell picked up the receiver in the other room, he hung it up.

After about ten minutes, Gaynell emerged from the back room. She came to the couch and told Flossy and Marion she had to leave for a while. She kissed them both and was out the door.

"Gaynell was gone for about an hour," Marion said. "When she came back, there were still a number of people milling about, but I noticed she was now no longer visibly upset. Instead, she was very business-like in her dealings with people. Handshakes took the place of hugs, and there were no more tears, merely a polite nodding of her head in accepting condolences."

Robert Hull arrived at the Moretta home to join his wife and mother-in-law. He had been on duty that day, and although Marion had called her husband at work, she had failed to reach him. Instead, she had talked with Robert's company commander.

"When my C.O. told me Betty Ann had been killed, I couldn't believe it," Robert Hull said. "I was in shock."

The commanding officer had his driver bring Robert to the Moretta home. As Robert exited the jeep and began walking up the walkway, two other gentlemen who had also just arrived at the residence joined him.

"I saw two men get out of a police car," Robert said. "One was in a suit, the other in uniform. We reached the walkway to the house at the same time, so I extended my hand to let the men pass. We reached the door, and the uniformed officer knocked.

"Nick opened the door, greeted the two police officers with a handshake, and then pointed to Gaynell. After the men had stepped into the house, Nick turned his attention to me and engulfed me in the type of hug reserved for family; then he escorted me to Marion and Flossy.

"I held Marion in my arms for a while and just let her cry. I knew how close she was to Betty Ann, and while I had not known Betty Ann for as long, I, too, was feeling the pain of suffering her loss."

In the meantime, Gaynell Moretta and the two men from the Los Angeles Police Department talked in the living room for a very brief moment; and then disappeared into a room in the back of the house. About five minutes later, the men emerged; and were escorted to the front door by Gaynell, where she exchanged handshakes with them as they left the house. She then returned to her position on the couch between Flossy and Marion, and again sought comfort in Flossy's arms. Nick had resumed his telephone screening duties and did not come to Gaynell with any calls for about half an hour.

Marion: "Nick took a call, placed the receiver down on the counter, and then came to the couch, where Gaynell was sitting between Mom and me."

"Thad Brown," Nick said to Gaynell in a hushed voice. Like with the call from Archie, Gaynell rose to her feet and went into one of the back rooms to talk with more privacy.

"I knew the name 'Thad Brown,'" Robert Hull recalled. "He was a big mucky-muck with the LAPD. We all knew Gaynell still had ties with the department, but I think when I heard the name 'Thad Brown,' I finally came to realize just how strong Gaynell's ties were."

Thad Brown was a member of the LAPD whom Gaynell had met during her days with Franklin Shaw. Brown's career began in 1926, and by 1947, he was one of the Los Angeles Police Department's deputy chiefs.

"Thad was a very good friend," Gaynell once said. "He was a good man and someone I knew I could count on if I ever needed anything. On September 13, 1947, I needed Thad's help, and like the friend he was, he came through for me. I had met with Thad earlier. His call was to just put my mind at ease about a few administrative things concerning Betty Ann's death."

After a few minutes on the phone with Brown, Gaynell once again reappeared in the living room. This time, instead of leaving the house, however, she made her way back to Flossy and Marion, where she again snuggled into Flossy's bosom.

"Gay, you alright?" Flossy asked, tightening her grasp around Gaynell's shoulder.

"No matter how long I live," Gaynell said, "I'll never be alright again."

Florence Clark stroked Gaynell's hair, hoping to bring some comfort to her friend. It worked. A few minutes later, Gaynell was asleep in Flossy's lap.

Chapter Twenty-Three
Propagation of a Murder Mystery

The loss of a child for any reason is tragic enough, but when that grief is brought about by a murder or a suicide, the situation becomes even more heartbreaking. Make no mistake, Archibald and Gaynell loved their children and were devastated by the tragic events of September 13, 1947. However, despite their grief, the two family heads also realized the additional misfortunes their families would endure if it were revealed that Robert Crosbie MacDonald was responsible for the death of Benjamin "Bugsy" Siegel.

While Bob MacDonald was alive, nothing seemed to connect him to the Siegel killing. After all, MacDonald was the son of Archibald MacDonald, one of the most prominent members of Southern California's aristocratic society and a key member of one of the most prosperous companies in the world. Bob MacDonald's mother-in-law was a former civil servant, and flourishing business-woman and MacDonald himself was the father of two beautiful children, had an attractive wife, and seemed to have a wonderful life ahead of him.

Once MacDonald killed his wife and then committed suicide, however, someone in the Los Angeles Police Department should have raised the question that the MacDonald murder/suicide and the Siegel case had more than a few things in common. Ironically, or as this writer claims, by design, despite the major red flags linking both crimes, no one—not the police, nor the press, nor anyone half-way curious—ever thought to look into the remote possibility that the Siegel and MacDonald murders could have been connected.

Why not? Simple answer! Archie MacDonald and Gaynell Moretta had the combined economic, political, and social clout to cover up Robert MacDonald's involvement in the crime.

There were four major red flags, which could have allowed police to speculate that the Siegel murder and the MacDonald murder/suicide were related. One, the weapon of choice to kill Ben Siegel was a 30-caliber carbine rifle; the weapon of choice used in the MacDonald murder/suicide was a 30-caliber carbine rifle. Two, the crimes happened within three months of each other—Siegel in late June, Betty Ann in mid-September. Three, the murders were committed within two miles of each other—1.8 miles to be exact. Four, Bugsy Siegel was connected to Jack Dragna. Betty Ann MacDonald was connected to Jack Dragna through her stepfather, Nick Moretta.

"Los Angeles in the 1940s wasn't like it is today," Robert Hull once said. "People of consequence, such as Howard Hughes, Archie MacDonald, Gaynell Moretta, Jack Dragna, and Bugsy Siegel, had the opportunity to know one another. Hell, they were all connected through Shaw, City Hall, and a social calendar that had to cause their paths to cross at more than a few functions."

* * * * *

Upon hearing that his son had murdered Betty Ann and then committed suicide, Archie MacDonald suspected the worst. Even though he was consumed with anguish, he was also keen enough to realize a situation existed that required his quick and quiet care.

Archie had been down this road too many times before with Howard Hughes. Since he knew his son was involved in Siegel's killing, he also knew he was dealing with a state of affairs that threatened the sovereignty of his empire.

"Archie had some powerful contacts with the LAPD and in City Hall, but he knew I did as well," Gaynell once said. "I don't think it took him a great deal of time to realize that if he wanted to keep Bob's involvement in the Siegel killing on the hush-hush, I needed to be a part of the plan. If I had wanted to, I could have screamed for an investigation and I could have easily revealed to the world that Bob was Siegel's killer.

"Archie called me late in the afternoon on the 13th," Gaynell continued. "After making an obligatory apology for what had happened, he asked if I would meet him at his office downtown.

"'We have some things to talk about Gay,' Archie said. 'I think we should get together as soon as possible.'

"I agreed, and thirty minutes later, I met him at a downtown office of the Hughes Corporation. We worked out a plan of attack to handle the matter with as little fanfare as possible."

Gaynell was fairly confident that Archie wanted to meet because he knew of Bob's involvement in the Siegel killing, but she wasn't sure of that fact until she entered his office and was greeted by the MacDonald family patriarch with a comforting embrace.

"I knew when Archie was holding me in his arms that he knew Bob was involved in the Siegel matter. He was shaking as if he had something to say, not because he was upset his son had killed my daughter or that Bob was dead."

Gaynell's instincts proved right. As Archie broke the embrace, he looked at Gaynell with concern.

"If we're going to prevent a bad situation from getting worse," he said, "we need to work together on this."

Archie studied Gaynell for a moment, assessed the situation, and then came to the point. "What do you think is going to happen if people find out Bob killed Siegel?" he asked.

Archie knew Gaynell had probably known about Bob's involvement in the Siegel murder before he did. He also figured he would have pissed her off had he decided to lie and deceive her in a cat-and-mouse game of who-knows-what. Cut to the chase was Archie's style and that was exactly what he did.

"We have to ask ourselves one fundamental question, Gay," Archie said. "What good will it do to have Bob identified as the murderer of Benjamin Siegel?"

Gaynell had already given that question some serious thought, and like Archie, she knew the answer.

"If Bob is exposed as Siegel's killer, we'll become social outcasts," Archie continued. "Will it bring Betty Ann back? Or Bob? Will it take away the pain you're feeling? Or mine?"

Archie was preaching to the choir. Gaynell had worked hard to achieve her position in society. She was living the life she had always dreamed of, and she was well aware of the fact that exposing

Bob MacDonald as Siegel's killer would cause her world to crash down upon her.

"Neither Archie nor I wanted our families' lives to come under the type of inspection that would have come about if anyone could have linked Bob to the Siegel murder," Gaynell once said. "Imagine the life of humiliation we would have faced.

"We had to do everything in our power to make sure no one ever discovered that Bob MacDonald was the person who had killed Bugsy Siegel. I didn't need a great deal of coaxing to enter into our little consortium of secrecy. No one could ever find out that Bob had killed Siegel."

Even before funeral arrangements for their children had been made, Archibald MacDonald and Gaynell Moretta formulated a plan to keep Bob's involvement in the Siegel killing a *family secret*.

* * * * *

By 1947, Archie had been a twenty-five-year member of Southern California's most exclusive organization, known as the Breakfast Club.

"Archie was intimate friends with many of Los Angeles' most powerful and influential citizens," Marion Hull once said. "These people were not only business associates, but close friends, confidants, and business partners as well."

"One of Archie's good friends was Harry Chandler, the publisher, and owner of the *Los Angeles Times*," Gaynell said. "Through Harry, Archie had made a number of friends in the press, including William Randolph Hearst. Even though Chandler had died in 1944, Archie's twenty-year association with him gave Archie an in with the press."

Archie knew many of the same police and political figures that Gaynell did—men who would be more than happy to help a friend in need.

"Archie had deep, generous pockets and was the businessman," Gaynell said. "So his role was acting as the bank and being the politician. While working for Hughes, there were more than a few occasions when his ability to sweet-talk a person resulted in the reaching of the desired goal. This situation was no different."

Of primary concern to Archie was the public relations issue that the MacDonald murder/suicide presented. How does one portray a murder/suicide in as positive a light as possible? Archie MacDonald found a way.

"Archie and I met with the people from the press," Gaynell said. "We gave them the pictures to use with the story and the quotes we wanted to appear in the newspaper. The whole article was orchestrated."

"In many ways, the press release on the murder/suicide portrayed Bob MacDonald as a mere victim of a tragic life gone wrong," Robert Hull stated. "Look at the photograph of him used in the *Los Angeles Times*. Bob was shown in his dress uniform, hat cocked slightly and sporting a warm smile. A very All-American, apple-pie-eating type of guy."

The *Times* article talks of MacDonald's heroics in the European theater and his distinguished war record. He was portrayed as a man who came home a war hero but found himself unable to adjust to the pressures of a normal life.

"In the article, my quote stated that the couple's problems mioght have arisen from Bob's inability to find employment," Gaynell once said. "Bob's lack of employment was always a source of friction between him and Betty Ann, since the end of the war, but the bottom line was that Betty Ann alone had over $100,000 in the bank. If Bob had been willing to stop gambling, they were a couple who would have been financially set for the rest of their lives."

"For a number of years after the Siegel killing, every time a carbine was found in Southern California, the owner of the weapon came under the close scrutiny of the police and newspaper reporters," Robert Hull stated. "Speculation always centered on whether or not the weapon was going to prove to be the murder weapon in the Siegel killing. These newspaper articles were run on guns that were found in garages, or car trunks, or in Nebraska cornfields. Any 30-caliber carbine found, either on or off the beaten path, had a column of print written on its history. Yet when Bob killed Betty Ann using the same type of weapon, in a crime that happened less than two miles from where Siegel had died, I thought for sure someone would put two-and-two together. No one ever did."

"The fact of the matter was that not one police officer, nor one reporter, nor anyone in a position of power ever raised an eyebrow or even asked if there was a remote possibility that the two crimes could have been connected. Archibald MacDonald and Gaynell Moretta formed an incredible team. They had the connections, the money, the ability, the desire, and enough dirt on those in power to make it happen."

* * * * *

"It was amazing how many people Gaynell knew," Marion Hull once said. "She had contacts in City Hall, with the Los Angeles Police Department, and with the coroner's office well into the '60s."

Robert Hull: "Gaynell once said she knew more than two dozen civil servants who had survived the purge of corruption in the early '40s who shouldn't have. She claimed she was the one person from the Shaw era with enough insider information to bring down a number of very powerful men."

The day after her daughter's death, Gaynell went downtown and visited with several old friends in City Hall, including Thad Brown, chief of detectives with the Los Angeles Police Department, with whom Gaynell had talked the day Betty Ann had been killed.

"Thad was a man who was trying desperately to repair the image of the LAPD," Gaynell said. "A few years earlier, the department had purged over sixty members of the force on corruption charges.

"I knew of about thirty more officers who had started their careers using the Shaw spoils system and who were still with the department. I asked Thad how the careers of several of those men were going. Thad very politely updated me on the progress of each man he knew, while I provided him with background information on those he didn't seem to know off the top of his head.

"I asked Thad if he would do me a personal favor: to find it in his heart to close the investigation on what was essentially a very private family situation as soon as possible. I told him I wanted no formal inquiries into the matter by the LAPD, and I was pleasantly pleased when he agreed to my request."

What Thad Brown knew about Gaynell Moretta was that she was a woman who had insider knowledge. She knew who still had a hand in vice and rackets and which officers were as unscrupulous as the day was long. Brown also realized that the LAPD could not survive another scandal if Gaynell Moretta came forward and revealed what she knew.

"For the sake of argument," Robert Hull said, "let's say that Thad Brown was aware Gaynell was in his office to ask him to cover up Bob MacDonald's involvement in the Siegel killing. In essence, what was Gaynell asking for? Benjamin Siegel had been murdered. The bottom line was that Siegel was a gangster, a criminal of enormous magnitude, and by all accounts, one of the most ruthless men in Los Angeles. In addition to Siegel's character flaws, no one, not even Siegel's family, was putting any pressure on the police to solve the crime.

"On the other hand, naming MacDonald as Siegel's killer would have had enormous ramifications for two of Southern California's most prominent and politically-connected families. Siegel's murderer, Bob MacDonald, was dead. Justice had been served. No one seemed overly upset that Benjamin Siegel was dead.

"In the '40s, if the Siegel murder had been figured out, the officer who was responsible for solving the crime would have gotten a slap on the back, a handshake, and been back on duty before the ink had dried on his report. Did the police care if the Siegel crime was solved? Not at the local level. What local cops cared about were their careers. A number of high-ranking police officers knew Gaynell could have ended their careers if she had been motivated to do so."

After talking with Thad Brown, Gaynell was comfortable in her belief that the MacDonald murder/suicide would be an open-and-shut case. In the end, Thad Brown agreed to honor Gaynell's request. At least two-dozen other officers, a few deputy district attorneys, and half-dozen members of the coroner's office are glad that he did.

Thad Brown later served under William Parker, as the second in command of the Los Angeles Police Department. Brown had a very long and distinguished career, before committing suicide in the mid-1960s.

Gaynell's next call was to Coroner Ben Brown.

"After Ben expressed his condolences, I asked him if the death certificate could read a 30-30 rifle as the type of weapon used to murder Betty Ann," Gaynell said.

"'That was what killed her, wasn't it?' Ben said.

"I then asked Ben if an autopsy had to be conducted.

"'We have to conduct an autopsy, Gay. You know that. It's the law.' Ben's smile was telling, however.

"Ben and I had been through a great deal in our day, but even with our history, I still wasn't sure if he was willing to become a conspirator in a murder cover-up. I asked him if he would consider contacting me if anyone came to him and asked him for an autopsy report or ballistics report. He didn't ask a single question, but I knew he had things figured out. After all, how many murders were committed in the Los Angeles area with a 30-caliber carbine rifle as the weapon of choice?

"Ben gave a sigh. A moment passed, then came to me and engulfed me in a hug. 'If I get a call,' he said, 'do you really want me to get in touch with you? Or would you rather I just make the matter go away?'

"'Can things just go away?' I asked.

"'They will if they cross my desk,' Ben said.

"I thanked him for his friendship and left knowing if anyone were to make a request for the autopsy, one would be provided. If there were an inquiry for a ballistics report, it would be provided as well. I also knew neither the autopsy nor the ballistics report would have any impact on my situation."

Marion Hull: "Gaynell was a powerful woman. She had many of the city's top officials in her hip pocket. While I have no doubt she had incriminating evidence on those men, I also have every confidence she considered most to be her friends. Gaynell would have never blackmailed anyone unless she absolutely had to."

The coroner's office filed a generic report. F.D. Newbar, M.D., an assistant under Ben Brown, signed it. There was no jury, no inquiry, and no real investigation.

The cause of death for Betty Ann MacDonald: Hemorrhage—Gunshot wounds of the chest. The cause of death for

Bob MacDonald: Hemorrhage—Gunshot wound of the head. The nature of accident: Suicide or homicide, domestic difficulties.

Like the LAPD, the coroner's office considered the MacDonald murder/suicide closed. The weapon used in the MacDonald murder/suicide was returned to the family. No ballistics test was ever conducted.

* * * * *

A number of influential politicians, police officers, and members of Jack Dragna's crime family attended the funeral of Betty Ann Rockwell. Also at Betty's service were Florence, Harry, and Gene Clark, and Robert and Marion Hull. Dan Dailey, the movie star, was there, as was Betty Ann's good friend, Elizabeth Hoffman, a dancer whose father was the owner of the famous Red Car Line in Southern California.

As people paid their last respects to the spunky, happy-go-lucky mother of two, each and every one had to ask one fundamental question: Why? Why, at the age of twenty-four, did Betty Ann, whose only wish in life was to seek and find true happiness, have to be put to her eternal rest?

After Betty Ann's service concluded and the mourners began to disperse, Marion Hull remained behind for several minutes. Arranging the flowers on Betty Ann's grave, Marion wanted to have one last moment with her best friend. She thanked Betty Ann for their many years together and promised to keep her spirit alive with tales of their youth and their friendship.

As Marion reached the parking lot, she took one last look toward her friend and saw two men walking toward Betty Ann's grave from the east. She began walking back toward the gravesite, and as she did, she recognized both men. Archibald MacDonald and Howard Hughes had come to pay their last respects.

"Archie laid a single red rose atop Betty Ann's grave," Marion said. "Howard laid down a dozen yellow roses, removed his trademark hat, and then he and Archie both knelt and prayed for a moment.

"As Archie stood, I saw him wipe a tear from his face. Howard stayed on his knees for a while, and then gently touched Betty

Ann's gravestone. Howard stood beside Archie for a moment, and then the two men went back the way they'd come.

"I always knew Howard, and Betty Ann had a wonderful friendship. I only came to realize just how wonderful it was after I saw Howard caressing the inscription on her grave. There was just something telling about the moment. It was beautiful."

Chapter Twenty-Four
Cracks, Loopholes, and Other Messy Things

"When I heard Bob killed Betty Ann," Robert Hull said, "I became physically sick. I thought to myself, *What if I had spoken out about Bob's admission? What if I had come forward and told someone Bob had admitted to me he had killed Siegel? Would that have kept Betty Ann alive?* Then, when I found out Bob had used a carbine rifle to commit the crime, my guilt tripled. Jesus God Almighty, I gave Bob the gun he used to kill Betty Ann! Did I help facilitate this horrible deed?

"Gaynell and I talked the day after Betty Ann's murder. I told her that Bob had come to me a few days earlier and stated that he had killed Benjamin Siegel. Gaynell didn't even flinch. I told Gaynell that I was feeling guilty because I was sure if I had come forward and revealed the information, that maybe, just maybe, Betty Ann would have still been alive. I also told her that I had intended to talk to her about what Bob had said to me in regards to Siegel at a family get-together she and Nick had planned for Sunday the 14th.

"Gaynell told me I shouldn't feel any culpability in Betty Ann's death and the truth was that others knew about Bob's involvement in the Siegel killing long before I did. I didn't think I was the only one Bob had spoken to about the killing, but at the same time, I wasn't sure, especially since until that moment, I wasn't convinced he had been telling me the truth. In some strange way, discovering others knew the secret helped ease my own guilt—at least a little.

"I offered to go to the police and give a full accounting of what I knew," Robert continued. "But Gaynell thought for a moment, and then explained her rationale for keeping Bob's involvement in the Siegel crime a secret.

"She asked me if I would be willing to keep what I knew to myself. I said yes. I promised I would tell no one about Bob's statement regarding the Siegel killing, not even Marion. As far as I knew, Gaynell never told a soul about our conversation that day.

"A few days after Betty Ann's funeral, Nick asked if I would meet him at the Newport Beach Marina. I agreed. When I arrived in the parking lot of the Marina, Nick greeted me with a hug. We walked to the back of his car, and he opened the trunk. The duffle bag I had given to Bob was inside.

"Nick unzipped the bag and asked me if the two weapons inside were the ones I had given to Bob. They were. There was also another weapon, a machine gun. He pulled the bag from the trunk then led me down toward the dock.

"I asked him what we were doing. He told me we were going to get rid of the guns. We reached a medium-sized boat, stepped aboard, and Nick went to the engine and fired it up. As we headed out to sea, I realized that I was about to become wholly committed to keeping Bob MacDonald's involvement in the Siegel murder a secret.

"During the boat ride, Nick and I talked about the horrors of what had happened. I asked him if he thought Bob had cracked as a result of being involved in the Siegel killing. Nick nodded his head yes.

"Eventually, Nick speculated on why Jack Dragna had used Bob for the hit. He felt that Jack had used Bob because he needed someone expendable. Sooner or later, Siegel's killer was going to end up dead. Since there was no love lost for Bob by anyone who cared about Betty Ann, Jack felt that getting Bob involved in the Siegel murder was going to result in killing two birds with one stone. In many ways, Jack thought he was doing the Moretta family a favor. With Bob out of the way, Betty Ann could have led a full and happy life.

"We went out about two miles. Nick slowed the engines, then came beside me, grabbed the duffle bag that was sitting on the deck, and loaded it down with a heavy chain. He asked me to drop the bag over the side.

"I lifted the chain, rested the bag on the side of the boat, paused for a moment, and then looked at Nick. He was crying. Nick was a good-hearted man who probably never imagined his life was going to be filled with this much turmoil.

"I shoved the bag into the water. There were a few bubbles and then it disappeared.

At that moment, I realized that life as I knew it would never be the same. I was involved in covering up a murder.

"At the same time, I understood the reasoning for doing what I was doing. I never questioned keeping Bob's involvement in the Siegel killing quiet. I knew in my heart it was the right thing to do. Siegel was dead. His killer had met his justice here on earth when he'd killed himself. At the same time, I couldn't have imagined how life for Gaynell, Nick, and Betty Ann's children would have been if Bob had been named Siegel's killer.

"It was strange, but after that boat ride, Nick and I became much closer. We shared a secret—a deep, dark secret that was never spoken of again, but at the same time never forgotten by either one of us."

* * * * *

Even before the tragedy of September 13, 1947, Archie Mac-Donald's world was in chaos.

"Howard had been ordered to testify before the Senate War Investigating Committee," Archie once said. "They were questioning him in regards to his work for the Defense Department. Needless to say, it was a very stressful time in my life. There were several times in August when Bob wanted to talk. He had problems, but I never had time for him. After Bob did what he did, I couldn't help but look back on things and wonder, if I had only been more available to my son, maybe, just maybe, I wouldn't have had to attend his funeral."

Archie MacDonald's stress could explain his attempt to manipulate the death certificate of his son. It was a behind-the-back move that almost cost the family's consortium of secrecy to blow up in his face.

"The plan was to list Bob and Betty Ann's marital status as unknown," Gaynell said. "We were not one-hundred-percent sure where things stood at that point with the Church. So putting 'unknown' for marital status was a valid answer on a legal, public document.

"On Betty Ann's death certificate, in box six, which asks if the deceased is single, married, widowed, or divorced, as the provider of information; I listed Betty Ann's marital status as 'unknown.'"

"On Robert MacDonald's death certificate, in box six, Archie, as the provider of information, listed Robert MacDonald's marital status as 'widower.' It took me a while to find out what Archie was trying to do, and when I did, all Hell broke loose."

Technically, Archie was right. Bob had killed Betty Ann before he killed himself, so in some sick way, Bob MacDonald was a widower. However; Gaynell was not one to fool around with.

"Archie was attempting to protect his money," Gaynell said. "Ella MacDonald probably had figured out that if Bob had been declared a widower, loopholes in the California inheritance laws could have been manipulated.

"If I were granted guardianship of the children, I could have been prevented from seeking financial compensation from Bob Mac-Donald's estate. There wasn't a great deal of money left behind by Bob, but it was going to go to help raise the children, and Archie and Ella were getting all flustered thinking they may lose a small piece of their wealth. Jesus Christ, Archie was worth about fifteen million in the late '40s. It wasn't like taking care of the kids was going to put a damper on their travel plans.

"The situation reminded me of what happened to Renny's folks when Linnie Rockwell tried to protect their money from Lorenzo's first daughter. I shared with Archie how the Rockwell greed had destroyed their way of life. I assured Archie that if he didn't do right by our partnership, I would make sure the MacDonald family traveled down the same path of destruction that the Rockwell family had."

On December 2, 1947, Archie MacDonald changed the status of Robert MacDonald from "widower" to "unknown." The next problem was the Church.

Gaynell: "I was unsure of what Betty Ann had told the cardinal, but what I was sure of was that the Church needed to be tidied up. Archie was a staunch Catholic and had connections way up the line. He volunteered to take care of the things that needed to be done, and I gave him my blessing. I was not an active church-goer; Archie was."

In talking to a representative of the Church, Archie discovered that a clergy member who has knowledge of a crime could only disclose information to police when lives are in danger. Information disclosed during a confession or counseling is confidential, even after the death of the confessor. While Archie felt comforted by the Church's philosophy, he still made a very sizable donation to the parish where Betty Ann had sought her counsel.

In addition to paying the Catholic Church what was in essence hush money, Archie had also manipulated the Church into granting Bob the right to a high Mass—a situation that created problems with Archie's co-conspirator.

"The fact that Archie essentially bribed the Church into granting Bob high Mass privileges pissed Gaynell off," Marion recalled. "She was livid, completely livid!"

"The son of a bitch is an adulterer, a murderer. He commits suicide and still gets a high Mass!" Gaynell stated on the day of Bob's funeral. "How is that right? Especially when my baby girl is only given a low Mass?"

Marion: "Betty Ann wasn't a staunch Catholic, so it probably wouldn't have mattered to her if she received a high Mass or a low Mass. Gaynell just needed something, or someone, to release her frustration on.

"More than anything, she was probably angrier with the fact that Archie went behind her back. Archie claimed that, with the Church granting a high Mass to Bob, they were saying he was a good soul gone bad. In addition, the high Mass showed that the Church was supporting the family belief that Bob's behavior was a manifestation of the personal duress he suffered as a result of his war experiences."

Gaynell wasn't impressed with Archie's explanation, but for the good of the order, she let her anger go. Despite a few close calls, the cracks in the conspiracy had been sealed, the loopholes brought together, and all the messy things cleaned up. The shroud of secrecy had been spun and laid into place. Archie MacDonald and Gaynell

Moretta had, in essence, covered up one of the most talked-about gangland murders of the twentieth century. If you don't think money and power can influence police and politicians – Think again.

Chapter Twenty-Five

Revenge, Hughes-style?

Speculation on why Howard Hughes came to Las Vegas has as many theories as the Siegel murder. For the most part, however, the number one belief is that Hughes saw Las Vegas as an opportunity to turn a profit. Hughes invested 85.5 million dollars and expected to make four dollars for ever dollar he spent. When all was said and done, he reached his projected profit margin and then some.

While Ben Siegel is given credit for being the father of Las Vegas, Howard Hughes is given credit for ending mob rule in Sin City. In effect, when Howard Hughes came to Vegas, organized crime lost the child Ben Siegel had given birth.

Hughes believed the development of industry and culture would allow Las Vegas to become the new-age boomtown. Many people thought his goal was to rid the town of gambling and make Las Vegas respectable. Nothing was further from the truth. What many people didn't know was that Hughes was working with Nevada's then-Governor Paul Laxalt to get legislation passed to open the gaming industry to public corporations. He wanted to own first a town, then a governor, and eventually a president. He came very close. Like Siegel, Hughes knew that if Las Vegas became a respectable, industrialized city, it would mean growth, which would generate millions of dollars for the gaming trade.

"Howard knew anyone who had a piece of the pie would make a fortune," Archie once said. "So he set out to convince six syndicate bosses that the good old days of Vegas were coming to an end and that their only chance at turning a final profit was to sell him their casinos."

On March 31, 1967, Hughes began his spending spree. He acquired properties from Moe Dalitz, Tony Cornero, Morris Kleinman, Tony Accardo, and Meyer Lansky. In order, Hughes took control of the Desert Inn, the Sands, the Castaways, the Frontier, the Silver Slipper, and the Landmark. In a fifteen-month period, he made the smartest bosses offers for their casinos that they couldn't refuse. When the smoke cleared in June of 1968, several of America's most famous mobsters had sold their properties to America's most famous billionaire. At the time, the mobsters thought they had made very lucrative financial deals. They would quickly discover how wrong they were.

When Howard Hughes gained a majority of the gaming interests in Las Vegas, organized crime's stranglehold on Sin City was over. The criminal elements that controlled Las Vegas believed that Hughes and his Ivy League associates would fail miserably with their business ventures. They were wrong.

After Hughes' organization took over their casinos, mobsters bragged that they were still able to take truckloads of money from the counting rooms without Hughes' people even knowing. Archie MacDonald chuckled at that notion.

"The idea that the Mob skimmed millions from Howard Hughes is ridiculous," he once told Gaynell. "It never happened! Those who claim it did are just attempting to cover up their stupidity for having an old man take away their most prized possessions.

"Howard taking Las Vegas from organized crime was like the class weakling beating up the school bully. When the fight was over, the bully had to have something to hang his hat on. By saying they were skimming money; they were looking for a way to save face. The class bully didn't want anyone to know the class weakling had kicked his ass.

"What pissed off most mobsters was that, even if they had bilked Howard for a few million dollars, he wouldn't have flinched. A few million dollars didn't matter to Howard, because by then, he was a billionaire. To Howard, what was a few million dollars, give or take?"

Long-time Hughes associate Robert Mahue probably summed up Hughes' involvement in Las Vegas best when he said, "For Howard, Las Vegas wasn't about money; it was about power and control."

Noah Dietrich, another long-time Hughes associate, agreed with Mahue's assessment, with a slight difference. "Howard's takeover of Las Vegas had nothing to do with money," he said. "It was something very personal. It was about something that he never talked about."

Archie MacDonald: "People can speculate all they want on why Howard Hughes went into Las Vegas. Only a handful of people know why he did what he did in the desert. I knew why he was there. Howard was trying to square things. It's nothing that needs to be boasted about nor bragged about. It was his way of making things right."

"Taking the lifeblood from organized crime was what Las Vegas was all about for Howard," Gaynell said. "One by one, he took away their children. He took what was special in their life. As time passed, the people who sold property to Howard must have felt like they had been victims of a sleght-of-hand trick. He took away their ability to make millions and millions of dollars. They had to be really pissed."

* * * * *

Hughes was aware of the Mob's contempt for Ivy Leaguers who thought they could come into Las Vegas and do a better job of running the gaming industry than they had. So it was sweet irony that the only man Howard Hughes ever agreed to sell a property to was an ambitious casino executive named Steve Wynn, a graduate of Pennsylvania University.

"In one of my last conversations with Howard," Archie said, "he told me he liked Wynn's ideas. While Wynn was unaware of Hughes' opinions of him, Howard felt Wynn held similar visions for Las Vegas to his own, and Howard liked that."

When Hughes uncharacteristically agreed to sell Wynn a piece of land near Caesar's Palace, the property provided Wynn with the capital he needed to springboard his career. He took the former Hughes holding and sold the property. With his assets from his deal, he went on to develop the Golden Nugget, the Mirage, Treasure Island, and several other modern-day Las Vegas super casinos.

"Mr. Wynn never knew Howard Hughes' reasons for selling him that piece of property," a Wynn representative stated to this author. "Mr. Wynn has always assumed it had to do with finance and development strategy. If Mr. Hughes sensed Mr. Wynn shared his dream for a metropolitan Las Vegas, Mr. Wynn didn't know about it."

Maybe Steve Wynn, in the late 1960s, didn't know he was destined to become the leading corporate holder of properties in Las Vegas. Perhaps he couldn't see how grand his future was. Maybe, just maybe, Howard Hughes did.

Howard Hughes wanted Las Vegas to become a growing, thriving, respectable community, free of mobster associations. In his mind, by selling Steve Wynn a piece of property on the Las Vegas Strip, he was in effect securing his vision.

Steve Wynn's ascent in the Las Vegas gaming industry not only sparked a significant growth in the hotel and casino industry but also generated a boom in the overall development of Southern Nevada as a whole. In what could be seen as a Hughes-type rise to financial success, Wynn, more than any other person in Las Vegas history, was a critical figure in making Las Vegas a flourishing, thriving, contemporary, American city.

Regardless of what Steve Wynn or his people may have known at the time, he was a part of Hughes' plan for a successful Las Vegas. Is it ironic or by design that time has proved Hughes to be correct?

* * * * *

Somehow I doubt even Bugsy Siegel could have fantasized the Las Vegas of today. Imagine the disdain of those mobsters Hughes bought out if they could see the city now. The influence organized crime currently has in the town built by mobsters is considered minuscule at best.

Las Vegas has become one of the fastest growing communities in America, and the Hughes Corporation is the third largest corporation in the state. In 2002, Las Vegas had 38,000,000 visitors. Clark County's revenue, just on gambling alone, was 7.8 billion dollars. That's billion with a B. If you listen to the people of Las Vegas, Howard Hughes is still the man who is given credit for placing the city on the economic boom it is experiencing today—not Bugsy Siegel!

AUTHOR'S NOTES

When I first decided to write this book, I assumed my motivation to complete my task would come from a burning desire to reveal to the world the identity of the man who murdered Benjamin "Bugsy" Siegel. Do I believe that Bob MacDonald killed Benjamin Siegel? You bet I do! Do I believe the collective lives of Archie MacDonald, Gaynell Moretta, and Howard Hughes allowed Bob MacDonald's involvement in the Siegel killing to be kept hidden from the world? You bet I do. Do I believe my father wanted me to reveal our family secret merely to solve the riddle of who killed Bugsy Siegel? Without question...No!

As I came to discover, the story I have written has little to do with solving the Siegel killing and everything to do with learning about my family. Because of the journey my father sent me on, I can now remove a stack of old newspaper clippings and photographs from a medium-sized cedar box and tell my family who the people are in every picture. By mere chance, the story these pictures tell removes the shroud of secrecy that was put in place over one of the most famous murder mysteries of the twentieth century.

I am sure there is more to this story than what I have presented; in fact, I would venture to guess there is much, much more to the story. Maybe one day, when this story gets out, more people will step forward with information that will shed an even brighter light on this incredible tale. Who knows we may even have to write another book.

ABOUT THE AUTHORS

Warren Robert Hull

Warren Robert Hull was born in Tacoma, Washington, to Marion and Robert Hull. In the early sixties, his family moved to the greater Los Angeles area. After graduating from High School, Warren went on to earn his bachelor's degree from the California State University at Fullerton and his master's degree from Adams State College. In the early 1980s, Warren served with the Naval Security Group and was attached to the National Security Agency (NSA). After a long career in education, in 2007, Warren accepted a position with the Clark County School District Police Department, where he currently serves as an Executive Assistant to the Chief of Police.

Warren and his wife Annette reside in Las Vegas, Nevada, and are the founders of AnnWar Productions and the Las Vegas International Film and Screenplay Festival. The couple has three documentary films to their credit; *A Band To Honor- The Story Of The USS Arizona Band, From USS Arizona Survivor To Unsung American Hero – The Lou Conter Story* and *The Man In The Middle*, which details the unlikely friendship of an immigrant from India (Sonny Jani) and a retired professional football player (Mike Webster) and their journey into the unknown world of the disease chronic traumatic encephalopathy (CTE).

Michael B. Druxman

Show business veteran Michael B. Druxman has written the screenplays for seven motion pictures, including *Cheyenne Warrior* with Kelly Preston, *Keaton's Cop* with Lee Majors, Abe Vigoda and Don Rickles, *Dillinger and Capone* starring Martin Sheen and F. Murray Abraham and *The Doorway* with Roy Scheider, which he also directed.

He is also a prolific playwright with five produced works to his credit. His one-person musical play, *Jolson*, has had productions in several U.S. cities. Additionally, he is the author of ten published books, including *The Art of Story-telling*, a "how to" book on writing that is used as a text in several colleges, plus mystery/suspense novels, *Nobody Drowns in Mineral Lake*, *Jackie Goes to Dixie* and *Dark Chasm*.

www.ingramcontent.com/pod-product-compliance
Lightning Source LLC
Chambersburg PA
CBHW070358100426
42812CB00005B/1547